It's
Not
About The
Belt

You Don't Need a Black Belt
to Live Like One

Master Chris Berlow

Visit our website at www.itsnotaboutthebelt.com

Published by TechPress, Inc.
6611 N 64th Place, Paradise Valley, AZ 85253
www.techpresspublishing.com

ISBN: 978-0-9837339-2-8

First Edition: November 2012

Cover design, photo editing and layout:
Offir Kilion, NY Photocraft
www.nyphotocraft.com

Tree photos by Chris Berlow

FOREWORD

There are many "how to" books in the martial arts, but books about martial arts character and values are few and far between. Books that teach how the character and traditional values built through the practice of the martial arts can be applied in everyday life are fewer still. *"It's Not About the Belt"* does just that – it teaches how anyone – of any age or sex, students of the martial arts and nonstudents – can adopt these characteristics and values to build a better life.

I was first introduced to Master Chris Berlow a few years ago by one of his students, a delightful lady named Marilyn Kretzer. Chris had co-authored a book, *YOU Have Infinite Power*, and was in need of some assistance with its publishing. Marilyn, who knew me through TechPress, referred Chris to me. *YOU Have Infinite Power* introduced the T.R.A.N.S.F.O.R.M.A.T.I.O.N. Doctrine, a process, for reinventing and reinvigorating one's-self and establishing a mindset conducive to achieving success. From the moment I first read the book, I was fascinated. The doctrine, at least to my mind, had its basis in the fundamental principles of martial arts, resonated with my personal philosophies.

As I got to know Chris Berlow and his family, it became very clear that he not only talks the talk, but walks the walk. His martial art credentials are exemplary, with many national awards – not only as a competitor but as a teacher of the martial arts. He has dedicated his life to the practice and teaching of martial arts and, significantly, demonstrates those values in his everyday life. He is unrelenting in applying himself to his "Worthy Ideal" – to impact the masses to live a life filled with health and happiness through the martial arts.

Chris has been blessed by the tutelage and guidance of many of the foremost Masters and Grandmasters in Tae Kwon Do. In *"It's Not About the Belt"*, Chris explains how to apply the values and lessons that he has learned over a period of three decades, to improve your everyday life.

As Chris points out, you don't have to be a black belt to adopt the martial art mindset and values. In fact, even if you have not had any training in the martial arts, you can benefit from those disciplines and values. Those that have trained in the physical aspects of the martial arts have a definite advantage, but that does not mean that those who have not had that privilege cannot learn them, adopt them, and take them to heart.

When "martial arts" are mentioned, most people think in terms of physical self-defense. A few years ago, I was sitting in a conference room with a new client. "I understand that you are a black belt," she said.

"Yes ma'am," I responded.

"So, have you ever had to use your martial arts?" She inquired, asking a question that I encountered on a regular basis.

"Every day," I answered, quite truthfully.

Her eyes grew big. She was clearly imagining me dealing with some physical confrontation de jure. I had to smile. Tapping my head, and my heart, I explained, "The martial arts are much more than just punching, kicking and grappling. They involve a specific mindset, a philosophy and code of conduct. I use those every day."

This anecdote is relevant because, although my martial art credentials are respectable, they are, shall we say... ancient. As my daughter so succinctly put it, I was born in the first half of the last century. While I hold multiple black belts of various degrees in Tae Kwon Do (from both the World Tae Kwon Do Federation/Kukkiwon and International Tae Kwon Do Federation) and in Hap Ki Do, school, they were awarded back in the 70s and' 80s. I hold an AAU state sparring championship from well before many of you were born, and a slew very dusty trophies. And, while I have served in years past as a senior instructor, and briefly had my own informal school, I have not formally trained since beginning a series of joint replacements about 10 years ago. The point is that even though, at present, I am not actively practicing the physical aspects of the martial arts, the disciplines and values that I learned clearly shape the way that I live my life: I use martial arts discipline and philosophy every day. You can too – whether or not you are a student of the martial arts.

The basic tenants of Tae Kwon Do are: respect, integrity, perseverance, self-control, and Indomitable Spirit. As Chris points out, these tenants are the ideal value system to guide you as you make your way through life. Think about it, if more people lived by those simple principles wouldn't our world be a better place to live? Imagine a society where morality and integrity are the foundation of all business endeavors, and the rule for all relationships is courtesy, respect, and self-control. Would your life and economic situation improve if you had an abundance of confidence and perseverance to give you the strength to follow through with your dreams and aspirations?

"It's Not About the Belt" will teach you how to use the philosophy and tenants of the martial arts as a guide in your everyday life.

An additional message to those of you that are students of the martial arts: It truly is not about the belt; anyone can buy a belt. "Black Belt" is a mindset of excellence that one lives by. It is what goes into earning the belt that defines one as a martial artist. It is the years of overcoming challenges while maintaining a positive mental attitude and that fact is what gives someone the right to say they are a "black belt".

There is a great quote that I once heard about the lifespan of a martial artist.

"The beginning student in most martial arts disciplines wears a white belt that, according to tradition, signifies innocence. With the passage of time, the belt becomes soiled from handling and use. The darker colored belts signify the next stage of learning. As more time passes, the belt becomes darker until it is black—the black belt stage. With even more use the black belt becomes frayed, almost white, signifying that the wearer is returning again to innocence."

A Zen Characteristic of Human Perfection

Master Berlow often quotes his Grandmaster, Grandmaster Byung Min Kim, who puts it much more succinctly:

"You know how much you know when you realize how much you don't know".

As you mature as a martial artist and black belt, you attain the "innocence" of the realization that training in the martial arts is an eternal path, imbuing your spirit with the tenants, a path that could ultimately lead to forever happiness. The point, driven home in *"It's Not About the Belt"*, is this: you do not need to wait until you are awarded a black belt to begin to live like one.

In good health and Martial Arts Spirit,
Michael A. Lechter

DEDICATION

I dedicate this book to two very special people whom I miss very much.

My mother; Ann Delano, who was the epitome of perseverance with all she had overcome in her life. She was the true representation of unconditional love to all who were close to her heart. Wow, do I miss her. When there is a challenge, I look up to her and believe that she still guides me through whatever stands in my way. Miraculously, I always prevail.

And to my original Taekwondo Instructor, Grandmaster Robert Connolly, who introduced me to Taekwondo when I was 13 years old and sparked a passion that still exists. He was like a father to me at a tumultuous time in my childhood into my adulthood. He gave me the first opportunity to become a professional martial artist and I am very grateful for that.

ACKNOWLEDGEMENTS

There are numerous people that I would like to acknowledge. These people have helped me over the years to become the Martial Artist that I am today. The list is numerous and is definitely not in any level of importance or significance by any means.

First, I have to acknowledge my family. My wife Kathy, who is always standing by my side and supporting me all the way, no matter how crazy the adventure is. I love her with all of my heart and as she knows, "Everything I do, I do IT for her."

My five children, Brandon, Andrew, Timmy, Stefanie and Kimberly. Many of them share my passion for the Martial Arts and all of them share my passion for personal development. They make me extremely proud and I love them from the bottom of my heart. They all are the reason why I do what I do, and they inspire me everyday to be the best husband and father I can be.

To my brother John, and sisters Mandy and Lynda, who have been super supportive over all the years. It is always awesome to know that we have each other's back no matter what the situation.

To my father, Curt (Grandpa), who has instilled in me a work ethic that is second to none. It is his support and guidance that has enabled me to work as hard as I do.

I would also like to acknowledge my Taekwondo Family. First and foremost, I would like to acknowledge Grandmaster Byung Min Kim, whose teachings have impacted my life extensively. He has given me such clarity in the roles and responsibilities of being a professional Martial Artist such as how it is our responsibility to pass on and expand the values of Taekwondo to elevate the persona of martial arts professionals, so that it can be a viable career option for future generations. He has instilled in me the sense of accountability. To constantly continue to train and improve so we can be the living examples of the martial arts values.

To Grandmaster Ed Ciarfella, who has been a great mentor and friend to me, and is a huge contributor to the person I am. I am very grateful for all the wisdom and knowledge that he has given me over the years. His vision and passion is second to none and I have tremendous amount of respect for him.

Master Paul Melella, who has been my training partner from the start and like a brother to me. I respect and care about him with all of my heart and look forward to a life-long friendship with memories that will continue to grow for the rest of our years.

To Master Joe Badini, my other training partner and best friend. His commitment and support to our friendship have been invaluable and I hold him in such high regard.

To Master Paul Edwards who is a great friend. I am truly appreciative of the time we spend together and the guidance he gives my son.

To Master Vinny Bellantoni, Master Occelli and Master Giacovas who have been the greatest supporters over the years and the world's best students. They share my passion and love for Taekwondo and impacting others.

To the rest of my instructors and staff: Inst. Parchen, Mrs.

Rocco and the entire UMAC team. Thanks for doing what you do so I can do what I do.

To Sensei Joe Joe. We share so many passions together along with a shared love for Martial Arts. I have tremendous respect for you and look forward to years of training together.

I would like to acknowledge my son, Sr. instructor Timmy Berlow, who has become a great Martial Artist and leader to so many at such a young age. I am extremely proud of the instructor he has become and know he will be a great Master some day.

My Empowered Mastery Team of Rick Wollman, Nick Palumbo and Paul Melella, who share the same passion of making a positive contribution to others and have given me the opportunity to spread the values that I believe in so strongly to a greater reach. I have such great respect, appreciation and gratitude for your friendships and look forward to a long prosperous career together. It is Empowered Mastery's worthy ideal to: *"Inspire and impact professionals and entrepreneurs to achieve ultimate success personally, professionally, physically and spiritually so they could live a life of passion and purpose."* Thank you from the bottom of my heart for the opportunity.

Last but certainly not least, I would like to thank all of my students and clients whom have entrusted me to guide them on this martial arts journey. I do not take this responsibility lightly and you all have my commitment to continue to set the example and lead you through your life's journey.

Cam Sah Ham Ni Dah

Contents

INTRODUCTION

I am teaching a class in self-defense techniques at United Martial Arts Centers [UMAC] in Briarcliff Manor, New York. I notice that the students, who are between the ages of seven and twelve, are not performing at their best, but merely going through the motions. I call a time out, and ask them to sit down to partake in an important discussion, one that will change their whole perspective of what it means to be a Martial Artist and a Black Belt.

I explain that as beginner students, we are training to become Martial Artists. We are learning about the five tenets of Taekwondo: integrity, perseverance, indomitable spirit, respect, and self-control. Our job is to put those tenets into our lives in whatever we do, whether we are in school, at home, at work, or at play, we are always striving to be the best we can.

The students are paying close attention as I explain what it means to be a Black Belt. A Martial Artist will put the principles into action, most of the time, living by those values and using them in everything he approaches. I then tell them a secret: "You don't need to be a Black Belt to act like a Black Belt." I continue: "You don't need to wait for the belt to encircle your waist. You can live by the Martial Arts precepts, because a black belt encircles your heart." I asked the class to demonstrate how a black belt sits. They all sit up really straight, backs erect and eyes focused forward. "See," I say, "you *do* have Black Belt character, even though you are only blue belts. That means you are on your way to becoming the best Martial Artist and person you can be."

Whether you are a child or an adult, you will benefit from the contents of this book. Open your mind and your heart, accept this information and put it into action. Hold yourself to the highest standards in all that you do. Hold yourself to the standards of a Martial Artist, the standards of a Black Belt!

The Martial Arts philosophy has taken our country and the world by storm. It is one of our culture's most popular activities for children and adults alike. Traditionally, people would train in the Martial Arts for the sole purpose of self-defense. As years passed, it was discovered that Martial Arts training offers tremendous benefits other than its physical aspects. The byproducts of constant discipline and structure are very similar to modern-day military programs. We notice something special about people who are or who were in the military. An advanced level of discipline, respect, honor and integrity is evident in the way they walk, talk and behave, earned through hard, vigorous training. What sets them apart is the Black Belt attitude, which can be used in our everyday lives. This is the subject of this book. We hope that whoever reads it will live their lives as Black Belt Martial Artists.

A Black Belt is a person who has dedicated much of his or her life to physical, mental and spiritual self-development through the Martial Arts. To obtain Black Belt level, one must apply and understand the physical aspects of the art. Each Martial Art has its own requirements and standards to achieve the level of Black Belt. The only way to tell a good school from a bad one is to see if it incorporates the physical *and* mental benefits of the Martial Arts – not just the physical. Every Black Belt in every type of Martial Art will have undergone significant training, which forms character.

Black Belt character is based on mental philosophies that are the foundation of the Martial Arts. These tenets have always existed but will not be able to be applied to the student's life, on a practical level, until after years of training. The mental benefits are a byproduct of the physical training. Modern-day Martial Arts programs emphasize the character traits of Martial Artists, which are achievable before reaching the Black Belt level. Since my background is in Taekwondo, I will base the mental aspects of that Martial Art in my teaching. The five tenets of Taekwondo are: *Integrity, self-control, indomitable spirit, respect* and *perseverance.*

...nes a true Black Belt when he can integrate ...s of the Martial Arts in his everyday life, and when ...e can use the five tenets as his personal set of rules to live by. When there is a problem, he will be able to identify how to handle the situation by applying these tenets to it. The goal of a Black Belt is to base his life on those values and stand by them at all times. The five tenets, in greater detail:

Integrity: The ability to do a great job both under supervision and when alone. A Martial Artist does not need to be watched over all of the time. He knows that what really defines integrity is not what he does when others are watching, but what he does when on his own.

Self-Control: I always ask my students to quote Peter Parker's uncle's last words, from *Spiderman*: "With great power comes great responsibility." Students must know that being a Black Belt entails great responsibility, physically and mentally. We develop enough power to seriously hurt someone, but we never misuse that power. Mental self-control is the key to not sweating the small stuff. We develop the self-control to allow insignificant matters not to bother us.

Indomitable Spirit: A Black Belt will approach and fulfill all challenges and opportunities with excitement, enthusiasm and energy. He will look at problems as challenges and setbacks as learning experiences. He will find the positive in every situation.

Respect: Respect is the foundation on which the Martial Arts are built. It is a responsibility of a Black Belt to show respect to everyone, including those he may not agree with. Respect begets respect.

Perseverance: Perseverance is essential in the Martial Arts. In order for one to become a Black Belt, one must show incredible perseverance and the ability to overcome numerous physical and mental challenges.

The goal of this book is to help beginning Martial Arts students gain a greater understanding of the philosophy. If everyone in our society lived the life of a Black Belt or a Martial Artist, we would all live together with much more harmony. Please take advantage of the information in this book and pass it on to as many people as you can to help make our world a better place. This book is designed for people of all ages, since everyone can benefit from the ancient principles of the Martial Arts.

❝*A black belt is nothing more than a belt that goes around your waist. Being a black belt is a state of mind and attitude.***❞**

RICK ENGLISH

❝*It's not whether you can or can't, it's how you are going to do it.***❞**

MASTER CHRIS BERLOW

CHAPTER 1

WE'VE GOT THE POWER

One major benefit you can receive through the practice of the Martial Arts is attaining enough personal power to achieve any goals that you may have. Personal power means taking charge of your life by making the best choices to help you become successful. This kind of power is infinite, but is also difficult to achieve. Each of us has the power to make our life whatever we want it to be. The most successful people take advantage of this power and run with it.

Take a look at professional athletes in America. Very few aspiring athletes will make a professional career of their sport. What makes those few reach the big time? What is it about them that are special? While every successful athlete has a unique story, they all share the common thread of *desire*. They have goals and aspirations and they are determined to accomplish them. The goals that they set are important and strong enough to guide the choices they make day to day. To pursue their dreams, they work hard when everyone else is resting. They choose to run that extra lap, to throw that extra free throw. They choose to push beyond everyone else in the field. Not many will become great in professional sports, but everyone can achieve the same quality of greatness in his or her personal life. The word sacrifice means, "to give up something of a lesser value for something of a greater value." For an aspiring individual, whether in the Martial Arts or any endeavor, there is always some kind of sacrifice along the path that leads to success. For example, parents will sacrifice of themselves for the benefit of their children. This happens all over the world, and in almost every species. Parents provide their children with the best childhood experience possible. This requires making sacrifices. Many moms will put their careers on hold to raise their children. They are sacrificing something of a lesser value, their career, for a greater priority, their children. For parents who have no choice but to work as they raise their children, they will sacrifice personal interests to spend time with their children. Same sacrifice in a different way.

As a Martial Artist, you sacrifice an old way of thinking for a new one. When you take on that Black Belt mindset, you will be giving up your old habits for a set of new ones. Destructive or ineffectual habits of the past are replaced by empowering habits, such as eating healthfully, having a positive attitude, showing respect to others, and pursuing both physical and mental training. These sacrifices may be challenging, but are incredibly rewarding as you live with positive values that will benefit yourself and those whom you care for.

All professional athletes have natural talent, a certain knack they discovered they had, and which they run with, full force. Most of us won't have the single-minded parental and tutorial encouragement, the trainers or support staff to keep us focused on our goal, so we must learn to make the right choices for ourselves, to help us achieve success in whatever we do.

Choice and Effect

I would like to tell a story of a person very dear to my heart, my mother, who is a living example of the theory of "Choice and Effect." As I write this book, she has just turned 66, and every day she lives is a miracle. She suffers from emphysema and COPD (Chronic Obstructive Coronary Disease). She can't breathe very well from years of smoking cigarettes. Her story goes like this:

She started smoking at sixteen, in 1956. Back then, it was definitely the cool thing to do. All the movie stars did it, and all the social role models did. The doctors endorsed it, and cigarettes were endemic in advertising. Back then smoking was touted as a healthful practice. People were unaware of the health risks that we know about now, the dangers that are verified by everyone like my mother who suffer and die from lung cancer and related diseases.

My mother regrets every day that she ever lit up one of those deadly cancer sticks. Everything seemed to be going all right for her until October of 2000. Although she smoked regularly, she still maintained an active lifestyle like that of any healthy woman of her age. For her 60th birthday, my brothers and sisters and I planned a big family reunion, with all of the grandchildren, to take a trip to Disney World. Our plans had to be cancelled because Mom suddenly had to spend a week in the hospital. For the next year, she was in and out of the hospital every few months. That was when we discovered about the COPD and emphysema. The doctors started pumping steroids into her, to help her breathe. Despite all of this, she still smoked.

Early one morning in February 2002, the phone rang. It was my father, who said that Mom had stopped breathing, and to come over fast. At my parents' house I found complete chaos. My brother, who is a paramedic, had just arrived; he knew the people bustling about my mother, who had stopped breathing and was in cardiac arrest. She was actually gone, but the EMS revived her, rushed her to the hospital, and put her on a respirator, which she stayed on for two weeks in Intensive Care. One of my sisters drove up from Maryland and another sister, who was serving in the military overseas, was flown in by the Red Cross. Mom's only way to communicate was by pointing at the letters of the alphabet printed on a board. Of course, later she didn't remember any of this, and after this traumatic experience, went home and continued smoking. It was an extremely challenging time for all of us, seeing our own mother suffer so much. It was just not real.

We'd assumed she'd be with us forever. She was so active, and was one of the most artistic people you could imagine. A baker and a master cake decorator, she once made a gingerbread village that was featured in *McCall's* magazine. The next year she made an edible carnival out of gingerbread, complete with a spinning carousel and a rotating Ferris wheel. One of her cakes, which sold for $12,000, was an exact replica of the Macy's building in Manhattan. And while raising four children, she also worked as a foreman on a construction job. Mom was Wonder Woman in every sense of the word, but now she couldn't breathe.

She continued to smoke and the doctors continued to pump steroids into her body. The problem with steroids is that while they help you breathe, they also weaken the bones. One day when she was lifting something, she felt a stab of pain in her back. She went to an orthopedic surgeon who said that her spine had been fractured and compressed. As in a domino effect, sixteen other bones fractured and now she was bedridden and in terrific pain. She couldn't breathe; and now she couldn't walk. She stood three inches shorter than before. We watched our mother deteriorate before our eyes. Why had this happened? Because she'd made a wrong choice when she was sixteen years old.

Her condition would improve slightly, and then worsen. It was clear that she never again would enjoy the quality of life she'd had before she turned 60. It was as if a switch had gone off and her body said: "It's over"; but she wasn't ready to give up. In 2004, she went into cardiac arrest again; and again the EMS brought her back to life in an ambulance. While in the ER that same day, it happened again. Believe it or not, she pulled through once more. She was sent to a rehabilitation center, where she was detoxified of all the medications in her system. She had to learn how to walk again, and after that, she was flying! She even started training in Taekwondo under me, and earned her yellow belt. Little did we know that she was still secretly smoking. When I found out, I placed pictures of her grandkids in front of her and asked her if she wanted to see them grow up. I hoped that her love for them would overpower her addiction to smoking. But the cigarettes were still winning.

In 2005 she finally did quit smoking. The lung damage was extreme and she was unable to maintain the lifestyle she wanted, no matter how hard she tried. Her longtime use of steroids had made her bones brittle. One day when she attempted to pick up a fifteen-pound package, her arm broke, just like that. All because she had smoked cigarettes for over forty years.

That same year, 2005, she was rushed to the hospital after yet another cardiac arrest. We joke that she has nine lives and still has four left; but she is using them up rather quickly. Again she was on a respirator for an extended period while they pumped in the steroids to help her breathe. She was under for so long that when the tube was pulled out, she couldn't walk. Her legs were paralyzed. It took over three weeks of rehab to be able to walk with a walker. For a time, she regained her ability to walk on her own.

As I write this book, it has been two years since she passed away. There is not a day that goes by when my siblings and I don't think of her. It's not only her absence that saddens me, but the pain she experienced in her last years. That stage of life is supposed to be "the golden age," full of freedom and enjoyment, but it ended up a nightmare. All because of her bad choices early in life, this destined her to an existence of extreme limitation and suffering. The positive outcome of this experience is that through sharing her story with you, maybe it will prevent nonsmokers from starting, and encourage smokers to quit.

The moral of my mother's story is that the decisions we

make today, directly and often indelibly, affect our future. My mother had chosen to smoke, unaware of the tragic consequences, and suffering now because of it. We must make the right choices to ensure our well-being. The right choices and the wrong choices both influence what becomes of us.

If you are in middle school or high school or a mature adult, your whole future is in front of you. There is nothing you cannot achieve in your life by making the right choices. Don't be tempted by negativity, peer pressure, or by what the superstars are doing. Listen to your gut and opt for that which will help you fulfill your dreams.

Act like a Black Belt, who looks at all situations and analyzes the effects of their decisions. Be aware of what you are doing and choose only that which will help you go in the direction you want. Remember, a true friend will help you achieve your aspirations, and not try to pressure you into something you shouldn't be doing. Black Belt character is making beneficial decisions that will help you achieve your dreams. Find friends who are like-minded and will help you, as you help them. Use my mother's story as a reality check to remind you that you do have the power to control your destiny. Unfortunately, in my mother's time, the knowledge that smoking was harmful was not available. Today, however, we have the knowledge. And knowledge gives us the power and the wisdom to do the right thing.

The decision to smoke is only one example of a bad choice. Any destructive habit or addiction will be counterproductive and potentially deadly; other examples are consuming excessive alcohol, overeating, engaging in reckless behavior, and indulging in the habit of being overly stressed. The point is, while you're young, be alert to temptations from peers and from advertisements whose business it is to sell you destructive products. Remember that the macho Marlboro Man, who sneered on billboards all across America, eventually died of lung cancer. Be on guard against any negative influence that may coerce you into becoming addicted to danger. A Martial Artist takes care of his well-being at all times.

"Man is made or unmade by himself. By the right choice he ascends. As a being of power, intelligence, and love, and the lord of his own thoughts, he holds the key to every situation.**"**

JAMES ALLAN

CHAPTER 2

BEING A GOOD FINDER

In our society, everywhere we turn, we encounter negativity. When you put on the evening news, you hear far more negative than positive stories, most of which are based on world and local problems: murders, car accidents, violence, natural disasters, financial crises. Once in a while comes a story that focuses on the good, but it is more often than not quickly swallowed up by pessimistic reports. So many films, too, dwell on tragedy and violence.

One of the most influential forms of media is the music industry. Thanks to MTV and VH1, music is as visual as it is musical, and the images portrayed are often full of negativity. Current rap songs, for example, promote out-of-control sex and violence and defiance of authority. This attitude is picked up by kids and creates trouble for the schools and families. It is "in" for young people to challenge authority at school, at home, and on the streets. Some popular artists even have lied about their background to promote a "Bad Ass" attitude. This is not what we need our youth to hear or see. Recently I was at a bas mitzvah where all of the thirteen-year-old girls were dancing and singing to an explicitly sexual song. This is what our youth are exposed to through the media today. Now, with iPods and personal video devices, there is less restriction than ever and it is much harder to monitor what is being listened to and watched. Another negative portal, of course, is the internet. There is nothing one cannot obtain from the internet. There are even websites to teach children how to go into a stealth program to surf the web undetected by their parents. All this promotes the negativity that is out there in the World Wide Web and, by extension, available to our children in "real" life.

With all of this negativity flying around and impacting so many people of all ages, it is not surprising what sort of content overwhelms the six o'clock news. One explanation may be *schadenfreude*, the tendency of people to feel better about themselves when they see others struggle or suffer. When there is some grim issue on the news, society's attention perks up because bad news makes people feel better by raising their self-esteem. This is not only misguided but dangerous, because the tendency then is that people will continue to seek out the negative to feel increasingly better about themselves. As people crave more negativity, in a vicious cycle the media is more than happy to deliver with more accounts of what is going wrong. I have chosen not to watch the news anymore, except to find out what the weather is going to be. And even then, when the weatherperson is describing a storm, I notice that he or she emphasizes how awful it is.

With the influx of all of this negativity, it is hard to stay positive. It is as if we are fighting an uphill battle against the iniquitousness of negativity. It is much harder to be a kid nowadays than it was in previous generations, which weren't exposed to such an onslaught of negativity. How do we stay positive and cultivate the strength to resist the influence of the media? The answer is to become a good *finder*. Every situation that arises in our lives has a positive side. Every argument, every injury, every challenge has a benefit; you just have to find it.

Let us take for example a Martial Artist who sustains an injury on his right leg. He is having trouble walking and it is difficult for him to kick. Focusing on the negative, he thinks about how he can't walk well, he can't kick, and how this injury is going to set him back and affect his other activities. The positive side is that the Martial Artist now will have greater appreciation for his body. He will prepare more carefully now, to prevent another injury. He will also have an opportunity to work the left leg to strengthen it while the right one is healing. The injury will also give the student a greater understanding of a crucial Martial Arts principle: *perseverance*, and how perseverance applies to his situation.

Let's take another example, that of one friend betraying

another. Of course, it is all too easy to focus on the negative: How could he have done that to me? He was my best friend. I loved him like a brother. I trusted him. So how can there be something positive about such a painful situation? Although it is hard to accept a relationship gone wrong, we can realize that it is for the best. You now know that your friend was not a true friend. You know it is time to move on to an authentically trustworthy friendship. Sometimes people stay in a relationship out of a sense of obligation. That becomes unhealthy for both parties. Having been betrayed, you know where you stand, and you are able to move on. You are clear and free, and that is a great feeling.

How do we act like a Black Belt when so many people around us are so negative? By becoming a good *finder*. Find the positive inherent in every situation. I have challenged students in class to come up with a bad situation and allow me to find the positive in it. I always have been able to counter any negative situation they came up with. One student mentioned the World Trade Center attacks of 9/11/01. The positive aspect of that disaster was that it united the nation with a flourish of American pride and compassion. All over one saw cars festooned with American Flags and, for a time at least, everyone was proud to be an American. Strangers helped strangers who became friends. People were open and generous with one another. The crime rate went way down because it united a country against a common foe. During one of the darkest times of the century, there was this positive outcome.

It is our responsibility as Martial Artists and Martial Arts Philosophers to find that silver lining in any and every situation. By finding the good, more good will come to you. In the law of attraction, like attracts like. If you always focus on the negative, negative actions will come to you. If you focus on the positive, positive actions will come your way. Therefore, we must find the good in all things and situations to attract more good energies to us. Be a good *finder* and you will live a happier and more fulfilled life. Shield yourself from the negative and don't get caught up in the media. You are stronger than that. You control how you feel, and you can choose to feel positive.

In the last chapter we talked about how we have the power to make the right choices that could affect our future. Now take that same power of choice and use it to find the positive in any situation. Most people look at things as problems; in the Martial Arts we look at things as challenges. A problem is a concern and a challenge is an opportunity. Turning the problem into a challenge that comes with an opportunity is only a different way of looking at the same scenario. If you could train yourself to be a good finder, you will live a more positive and gratifying life.

66*A pessimist sees the difficulty in every opportunity; an optimist sees the opportunity in every difficulty.*99
WINSTON CHURCHILL

66*It is during our darkest moments that we must focus to see the light.*99
ARISTOTLE ONASSIS

CHAPTER 3

THE "N" PEOPLE VS. THE "P" PEOPLE

We have just discussed the importance of being a good finder and what a challenge it is in this age of mass media, with all its negative messages. Negativity sells, so one sees it on every media avenue. As a result, many people are influenced negatively to live their lives in kind. They will not maximize their lives, but will succumb to the attitude that they are helpless in a life filled with what they perceive as evil. Such individuals live without purpose or reason and do what they must to get by, thinking that society owes them something, without knowing what they are supposed to expect. They look at the glass as half empty and are interested in other people's hardships to feel better about themselves. They are complainers who find it easier to complain than to take action and change themselves and their perceptions of life. Little do they know that they might take the energy they use in complaining and apply it to taking action to solve their problems and becoming happy and successful. These people we call "N" or Negative people. We all know people like this. They have the right to act as they please, but we cannot let their way of thinking affect ours. We have to be strong to withstand their unconstructive tendencies and not let them get us down.

Now let's go to the other side of the fence, to the "P" people, who are Positive. These individuals look at the same glass, which "N" people look at as half empty, as half full. They find the good in all situations, and that makes them good finders. They look at situations as challenges, not as problems. A challenge is something we are excited to face, while a problem is something that weighs us down. "P" people live a purposeful life and look at each day as a new opportunity, putting their energies into whatever is in front of them. They see matters in an expansive and more favorable light. They believe that they can make a difference in society by having an affirmative attitude. You will see them smiling and going out of their way to make someone else happy. They spend their energy not in complaining, but in finding solutions. These action people love to live and enjoy life fully. As masters of their lives, they do not allow anyone else to influence how they feel; they are in the driver's seat.

How do we avoid the negative and gravitate toward the positive? First, we should gain the ability, through awareness, to discriminate between the two types. As you go throughout the day, look closely at how people present themselves. Notice those who seem positive and those who seem negative. If someone is buying a cup of coffee without looking the clerk in the eye or thanking him, put him on the "N" list. Conversely, if he smiles at the clerk and says, "Thank you, have a great day," put him on the "P" list. Look around for "N" people and "P" people and mentally label them. A person walking down the street frowning angrily is an "N." Someone with a smile is likely a "P." After labeling everyone you come in contact with in a day, think about how you would prefer to be labeled.

The second step is to take some time to think about individuals in your life whom you would list as "N" and those you'd list as "P." Think about your friends and family members, and whether they look at the glass as half full or half empty. Who is up-beat? Who is often complaining? You probably will find that your friends are more like you, but that family members go either way. This is because you were born into your family, and you have acquired your friends. For negative relatives, do everything you can to try to lead them into having a positive attitude. Smile with them, make them laugh, and you will be helping them.

When it comes to friends, you have a choice. You choose who your friends are. Chances are your friends will be more like you than not. This comes back to the Law of Attraction, where like attracts like. Positive people will gravitate toward positive people and negative people will gravitate toward negative people. There is a good possibility that if you find all of your friends to be negative, you are probably negative also. Same rule goes with the positive.

Sometimes, as you get older, you may find yourself becoming more distant from some friends and becoming closer to others. This will depend on where you are in your life and where they are in theirs. For example, if you are in your twenties and married and have a child, while your best friend is going out partying every night, it is obvious that there is a difference in your respective priorities. You have responsibilities and have love with your family, and your friend is still going crazy. One state is not better than another, only different. You may find yourself gravitating to other young families, while your friend will drift closer to fellows who aren't ready to settle down. While it is fine to maintain a relationship with someone who is in a different stage, it should be positive. If the friend is unable to accept that and starts being negative, decide if the relationship is worth sustaining, or if it is time to move on.

When a friend has become negative and is a strong-willed, "N" person, try to save the friendship by helping him see things in a more positive light. Give him books, laugh with him, watch funny movies with him and dedicate time to helping him. If he does not accept your help and advice, it is time to move on. We all have a limited amount of mental and emotional energy. Eventually you will become drained if you keep trying without getting good results. Remember, people cannot change their ways unless they choose to. No one can do it for them. As the old saying goes, "You could take a horse to water, but you can't make it drink." You can expose your friends to the philosophies that help you to be successful and positive, but you can't make them live by them.

One thing to remember is not to feed the fire of negativity. In other words, when your friend is complaining, do not encourage the behavior by agreeing with him or giving him constant sympathy, for if you do, he will never get better. If you make him feel better temporarily, you will enable him to repeat the behavior. If a toddler falls down and the parents go crazy and bring a lot of attention to the fall, the child may cry and scream. If she falls down and the parents make light of it, she likely will have no reaction and will get up and keep toddling. With an extremely negative friend, you may find that the friendship is more work than it's worth. That is when you should decide whether to move on so that he does not bring you down. Remember, like attracts like and if you are positive and your friends are not, it is inevitable that you'll separate from them and move on.

Be a "P" person and surround yourself with "P" people and you will be acting like a Black Belt. A Black Belt always looks for the positive in every situation. He or she will be more than willing to help anyone, and will recognize whether the relationship is healthy or not. He will listen to and be guided by his instincts. He will not be influenced by negativity and is able to think things through to find the win-win result in or solution to every situation. That is the way of the Martial Artist, and that is the way you can be, too.

66 *I think it's important to get your surroundings as well as yourself into a positive state – meaning surround yourself with positive people, not the kind who are negative and jealous of everything you do.* **99**

HEIDI KLUM

CHAPTER 4

INTEGRITY IN LIFE

Integrity is one of the foundations of the Martial Arts and an essential characteristic of a Black Belt. Integrity means doing the right thing even when you are not being monitored by someone else. For example, in the Martial Arts, an instructor may ask students to practice a particular skill or technique. If the students practice well on their own, they will advance and have a chance at becoming great. If they don't practice, there is no way they will develop into a Martial Artist. A student who depends on the instructor for self-discipline shows that the student lacks integrity in the sincerity of his commitment. It takes commitment to go beyond what can be accomplished during class time. The instructor will not always be there to help the students, who must assume the responsibility of diligent independent practice. Students must have the attitude that they are in control of their success; it is their choice alone. As masters of their lives, only they will determine how great they become. You cannot become a Black Belt without integrity.

For one to have Black Belt character, integrity is equally

important outside the Martial Arts school. There's an old saying: "It is not what you do when you are being watched that counts, it is what you do when you are by yourself that defines your character." We must be true to our thoughts and our feelings. Do not project an image that you know is false, that does not represent what you truly are. Portray the image you see yourself as being. For example, if someone tries to impress his friends by doing something he feels unsure about, he should think twice before he acts, because once something is done, it is hard to take it back. If you are hanging around with a bunch of friends and start swearing curse words, you're projecting the image of a foul-mouthed, immature punk. In your heart you know that this is not what you are, and you know you should not be acting this way, but you do anyway. That is not having integrity, another word for wholeness, and is not behaving like a Martial Artist.

Integrity is doing what you say you will do, and, conversely, not doing what you say you'll not do. If you tell someone that you will call him back, be sure to do so in a timely manner. If you say that you do not indulge in fast foods, make sure you don't. It takes inner strength to stand by your words, and to do the right thing whether you are among other people or by yourself. Can you imagine a Martial Arts instructor encouraging students to practice hard on their own, but the instructor never does? Or for the instructor to tell students to eat healthfully, yet he frequents fast food restaurants? A Martial Arts instructor must walk the talk. That is true for everyone reading this book. If you want to have Black Belt character, you must walk the talk.

Integrity at work is the same as integrity anywhere else. To be successful in your company, do your best to fulfill all of the obligations of your profession. If your manager or boss gives you a task to complete, do it to your best of your ability. If your employer is out of town, do not slack off your work. This is as an opportunity to show your boss how valuable you are, and that he can trust that while he's away you can handle the job on your own, without him worrying about it. This is key to advancing in any field. If a co-worker lacks integrity, your great work still will come through. When you do the right thing, good things will come your way, in conformation with the law of attraction and the laws of the universe. The Sanskrit word for "right action" is *dharma*. It is the foundation of an ethical life.

Integrity is a must in healthy relationships too. Someone without integrity is not trustworthy and his relationships are doomed to fail. Integrity and trust work hand in hand and are the foundation of any healthy relationship. Be honest with your family and friends. Lying is destructive because it indicates lack of integrity, and it proliferates; one lie becomes more lies until the truth is irreparably muddied and lost.

This pertains to all of the relationships in your life, including the one you have with yourself. Your family, friends and co-workers must be able to trust and believe in you. For example, someone in a romantic relationship begins secretly to look around for another romantic encounter. This signals the loss of integrity and trust, and perhaps it's time for the betrayed person to move on. Whether you are dating in high school or in a marriage, you must always do the right thing; only then will you sustain lifelong relationships. No one wants to live among untrustworthy people. Be the best partner, the best friend possible, and you are bound to have wonderful relationships for life.

A Black Belt lives by his word. Integrity is his foundation, everywhere he goes, at all times. He is a living example of the Martial Arts principles in his home life, his work life, and his social life. Integrity is the key to success and the only principle to live by. Live the Martial Arts way and hold integrity as one of your essential values and you will be successful.

66Real integrity is doing the right thing,
knowing that nobody's going to know
whether you did it or not.99

OPRAH WINFREY

66Nothing is at last sacred but the
integrity of your own mind.99

RALPH WALDO EMERSON

CHAPTER 5

SELF-CONTROL IN LIFE

When children first enter the Martial Arts school to take classes, the first principle we teach is self-control. When a child is able to stand straight without wiggling, we praise that behavior. It is amazing to see students as young as four standing like a Black Belt. If a four-year-old can do it, I am sure just about any teenager and adult can too.

Self-control is another foundational principle of being a Black Belt. Self-control in the Martial Arts represents both physical and mental self-discipline. We develop physical control by coordinating our body through particular exercises. We develop the physical control of our body to execute techniques successfully and efficiently. Our mind sends signals to our body and our body does what it is told. Physical self-control is a total mind-body connection. This is achieved through lots of repetition and practice, and improves as time goes on.

Physical self-control will be required in physical confrontations. As a Martial Artist, you are trained to defend yourself in all situations. If you have been training regularly for years, you probably have developed a high level of skill and power. A Black Belt or a Martial Artist in a physical situation in which he must defend himself must do so with minimum force. In other words, if attacked, to be safe you must defend yourself (or someone who is weaker than you) by doing only what is necessary, but do not go out of control. After you've exhausted all possibilities to defuse the situation mentally, only then can you resort to physical force. Once you determine that a fight is inevitable, take care of it quickly and to the point. If you knock someone back and attain enough distance to get away, do not jump into round two. Stay safe and move on. That is the way of a Martial Artist. *Remember, with great power comes great responsibility.* Your responsibility is always to have enough self-control to avoid misusing your art.

More difficult still is mental self-control, the ability to control your mind to do what you want or need to do. Self-control of the mind requires having the inner strength to do what is appropriate in all situations. If you are in Martial Arts class sparring with a partner who is hitting you often, and if you are without mental self-control, you may yield to an uncontrolled, all-out assault. You will definitely lose and make a ton of mistakes in the process. The better way is to use self-control to direct your mind toward figuring out what you could do optimally in that situation. If you do that, you will grow from the experience. A Martial Artist will practice physical and mental self-control throughout his entire training.

A true Black Belt will demonstrate physical and mental self-control in and out of the dojang, at all times. He is always composed, in control of his emotions. He does not get overly excited, sad, happy or mad. An excess of any emotion indicates a lack of rationality. A Black Belt will come up with the logical solution to the problem, which is based on the principles of the Martial Arts. A Black Belt should remain calm and balanced in every aspect of his life to see things as they really are not how he imagines them to be. Black Belt self-control is achieved by developing a strong mind and a strong body to accomplish any action in any situation.

Self-control should be demonstrated physically and mentally in your everyday life. Physical control is achieved through repetition and practice. The world's greatest athletes have the ability to control their actions. After a ton of hard work and dedication, they have mastered the art of physical control to achieve greatness. Much mental control is involved, as well, athletes push themselves to practice harder and not quit when things get tough. That kind of mental control is vital in Black Belt philosophy.

The average person would benefit by developing mental

self-control. Much of the contention that exists in society comes from a lack of mental control. Many people react without thinking, and feel the need to shout to be heard, when they should be listening. We should control our reactions and clearly see the other person's point of view. An argument is nothing more than one person insisting that his point of view is the correct one. No resolution to a dispute ever will be achieved without mental control.

Here is a perfect example. If someone says something negative to you, you have a choice about how to respond. If you react in haste, without thinking, the situation could escalate into a strong confrontation. If you are able to control your reaction and analyze why this person is acting contentiously, you will probably be able to coast through the altercation without friction. Self-control is essential. In an argument, if tempers flare, no one wins. A Black Belt will try to find the path of least resistance and behave like a stream flowing through a rock bed. If there is any obstacle to the river's course, the water will find its way around it. Imagine a river stressing and fretting over a jagged rock in its way! A Black Belt will mentally do the same thing. Don't entertain the other person's negativity or anger. Let it roll right off of you and it will float harmlessly away. Find a solution to the situation that keeps you dignified and which calms down the opposition. If one has mental control, a solution will be found.

Self-control at work will give you the edge in your career. People are always looking out for their own interests and have no qualms about stepping on someone else's toes to get ahead. We have discussed the difference between the "P" people and the "N" people. In every field, there will be members of the negative type. The trick is to employ the old saying, "What goes around comes around." The one who is giving you a hard time will soon have a hard time himself. We also need to remember that people handle stress or pressure in various ways. As Black Belt students, we are working towards a life of calmness and tranquility. "N" people may not have that intention. We should have enough self-control to not let their negativity affect us. We control how we feel, our actions and reactions. If someone is giving you a hard time, simply smile and explain that you respect their opinion, but let's look at the situation from both sides and work together to find a compromise. Explain that we will work much better as a team then as constant adversaries. This kind of response is constructive. It conveys that you are willing to work together while contributing a solution to the friction. This attitude is definitely easier to advise than to enforce; however, we are looking to live with Black Belt character, which aims always to find a peaceful yet productive resolution to any conflict.

Self-control is also necessary in healthy and long-lasting relationships. Sometimes we take those who are closest to us for granted and not listen to them with enough attention. For a healthy relationship with your partner, always be willing to listen thoroughly to, and respect, what he or she has to say before responding. Sometimes intimacy or familiarity breeds a lack of patience and rationality. Even if you do not agree with your partner, it is only fair to see his or her perspective. Most people in troubled relationships have difficulty communicating. Have the Black Belt self-control to listen before you speak. As with every endeavor, what is required is hard work, practice and commitment.

There is no greater need for self-control than when raising children. The parents who are reading this book surely will agree. Children test you to the limits. Every stage of childhood presents a new set of challenges. Here are some tricks to help you maintain Black Belt self-control while teaching your children the values you set for them.

First is to remember that your reaction in any given situation will become their reaction to the same kind of situation. If you yell at them for some behavior you don't approve of, that is how they will react when someone does something to them which they do not approve of. Children seem to pick up on everything the adults around them do. There's a billboard advertisement that shows a close-up photo of an innocent young child, captioned by a caution: "If you yell at another driver, she is learning that lesson." Make sure you try to understand why your child did something before you get angry. When my oldest son was three and developing his potty skills, an interesting situation arose. One day while I was teaching at a Taekwondo school, my instructor said to me, "I have seen many things in my life, but why would anyone go poop in my mop bucket?" We had a good laugh about that, and I forgot all about it. The next time I brought my son to the school, he darted off somewhere. I looked all over for him, and found him in the bathroom where he was squatting on the yellow plastic mop bucket. Shocked and angry, I yelled, "What are you doing?" He looked up at me and sobbed, "I wanted to use the yellow potty." I took a step back and started laughing. As I cleaned up the mess, I explained that this was a mop bucket, not a toilet, and to use the toilet from now on. The mystery of the mop bucket pooper was solved, but I never did tell my instructor. I'd learned something important. My first reaction was to yell, but I understood the perfectly logical reason why my son had done what he did. Anger is not an effective teacher, but understanding is.

To demonstrate self-control to children is to keep the line of communication with them open at all times. This is as crucial as in the marital relationship. Your children must know that they can trust you, and that you trust them. They need to know that they can talk to you whenever they want or need to. Even when they have made serious mistakes, which are inevitable, they need to know that you will be there for them. Exercise self-control and respond without haste. Listen to their side of the story and don't pass judgment until you have. If you react by yelling, without listening, you put up a roadblock between you and your child. He may not want to talk to you at all from then on. Listening to your children and responding in a calm and relaxed manor does not mean that you will never discipline them. *Make sure you discipline the behavior, not the person.* And never do anything to impair your child's self-esteem!

Self-control can be applied in every aspect of your life. Black Belt control takes it to the next level. Remember to listen carefully, and search a little deeper to find a reason before you react. You will be happier and calmer for it, and others will look to you as level-headed and balanced. Think what the world would be like if every government around the world followed this mentality. There certainly would be far less conflict. If we as Martial Artists can reflect self-control in our lives, other people we come into contact with may follow suit, the Black Belt mentality will spread from person to person, and the world will be a better place to live in.

66 *He who controls others may be powerful, but he who has mastered himself is mightier still.* 99

LAO TZU

66 *You have power over your mind — not outside events. Realize this, and you will find strength.* 99

MARCUS AURELIUS

CHAPTER 6

INDOMITABLE SPIRIT

Indomitable spirit is the attitude with which we approach everything we do in our life. Whether he is at work or in school or at a club, a Martial Artist will maintain an attitude of excitement as he goes through the day. When a situation arises that needs attention, he approaches it as a challenge, not as a problem. Indomitable spirit is having a zest for life, an excitement for living and an enthusiasm about the future. Wouldn't it be great if we all had the type of philosophy that inspired us to live life to the fullest and take in everything around us with awareness and gratitude!

Take a look at a kindergartener waking up in the morning, ready for anything. She's always in a good mood and ready to plunge headlong into the day with boundless enthusiasm and excitement. She is excited, curious, and eager to tackle new opportunities. She loves school, and learning, and playing. This is the way we all should live. We can defy the restrictive ways imposed by society, and choose to do as we wish. That is indomitable spirit.

Let's take a look at the circles of life as they relate to

indomitable spirit. People go through many phases, and experience ups and downs as if they were riding a huge rollercoaster. The "ups" are the times we feel great spirit, and the "downs" are when we drag through our life, merely go through the motions of living. The peaks of the roller coaster represent moments of excitement and enthusiasm. Preschoolers and kindergarteners, as new learners, have a ton of excitement. Older children, transitioning into elementary or middle or high school, also experience the excitement of the new. Any apprehension or concern is met with natural courage and enthusiasm. And when they go to college, again they experience the new and exciting. A new bicycle, a new car, a new computer game, a new friend is greeted with eager pleasure. A new career, a first career, a first relationship garners exhilaration.

Challenges arise when people get older and become used to the things that once thrilled them. The novelty wears off and then come the gullies in the roller coaster ride. School, or the car, or the job becomes overly familiar. Even relationships sometimes lose their zing and result in separations. That which is missing is indomitable spirit, the highs of the roller coaster, the excitement about what's in front of you, the thrill to live, the determination to keep all things fresh and new.

A true Black Belt lives with indomitable spirit. Black Belt philosophy takes full advantage of all situations and circumstances as they come. The practitioner looks at every new day as a new opportunity to do great things. He has the zeal to pass his positive energy on to others. Black Belt philosophy means looking at every circumstance as a learning experience. When something goes "wrong," a Black Belt looks at it carefully, objectively, and analyzes it to determine how to learn from the incident and grow. A Black Belt will not dwell on an obstacle or allow it to weigh him down. A Black Belt does not avoid difficulties, but regards them as opportunities and a means of encouragement.

Black Belts are not afraid to laugh out loud and have fun. Life is supposed to be fun. When students are training to become Black Belts, we explain that they will be working hard to achieve that goal. There are many physical and mental requirements to accomplish to reach the rank of Black Belt. I explain the difference between hard work and working hard. Hard work is when you have to do something that is not fun, something you do out of obligation or responsibility. Examples are changing a tire, completing a report on a dull subject, or anything else that feels like drudgery or a struggle. On the contrary, working hard is doing something that you enjoy. Our Martial Arts training is definitely physically and mentally demanding, but we work hard at it because we love to do it. Marathoners love to run and work hard at it. It is not hard work to them. Indomitable spirit is taking the love of doing something in particular, and extending that love if working hard into all other areas of life. It is finding excitement in any circumstance. Someone who approaches life with excitement and the drive to succeed, who is willing to work hard to achieve it, has indomitable spirit.

No matter what you are doing or what age you are, the one who treats everything as if it were new will approach whatever task is before him with gusto. Think back to your excitement when you first met your husband or wife. Pretend each day is like the first time you met. Treat your job as you felt on your first day and you are filled with the enthusiasm to work hard to become successful. Imitate the great natural enthusiasm that most children have. Raise the bar and the standards of excellence in all areas to feel that what you have done is *awesome*. Whether it's Martial Arts training, your career, or your hobby, approach it with a "first time" attitude and you will appreciate it anew. That is indomitable spirit.

To keep up the indomitable spirit, focus on the positive and ignore the negative. In an earlier chapter, we talked about the "N" people and the "P" people. We have to ensure that we are the "P" type. In any situation that arises, focus on what went right about it. To fixate on what went wrong is dispiriting, and makes us lose the motivation to continue. Cultivate Black Belt character, approach each new day as if you were in kindergarten, and keep your focus on indomitable spirit.

66 *Strength does not come from physical capacity. It comes from an indomitable will.* 99

MAHATMA GANDHI

CHAPTER *7*

RESPECT IN LIFE

Respect is at the center of the Martial Arts and the premise that drives everything we do. It is the first principle new students learn in the dojang and they will practice it throughout their training and in their outer lives. This tradition is thousands of years old. Around 500 AD, a warrior class, called the Hwarang Do (Flowering youth) was established in the ancient kingdom of Silla, in Korea. The Hwarang Do initiated the true meaning of the Martial Arts. This warrior class was extremely skilled in the fighting arts and was experts in weapons and in hand-to-hand combat. What made this organization so uniquely enlightened was its code of ethics. Members felt that a high level of spiritual and mental strength was equal to having superior physical strength which actually depended on great mental strength. It is similar to the principles of Yin-Yang in Chinese philosophy; in Korea it is called Eum Yang. The symbol is composed of two mutually dependent elements. One element without the other is inharmonious and incomplete. The code of ethics inherent in Eum Yang was the foundation of their mental strength. This code has funneled into the **Five Tenets** and the **Eleven Commandments of Taekwondo**.

The Hwang Do philosophy was derived from nine virtues: humanity, honor, courtesy, knowledge, trust and loyalty, friendship, kindness, wisdom, and courage. The common thread of all of these virtues is respect. These nine virtues became the Hwarang Do Code of Conduct. They are:

1. Loyalty to your country
2. Obedience to your parents
3. Trustworthiness to your friends
4. Courage to never retreat from the enemy
5. Justice to never take a life without cause.

All of these standards are based on respect. First is respect for and loyalty to one's country. Then, obedience toward one's parents. In ancient Korea, people esteemed their elders. Then, they practiced trustworthiness, loyalty and respect for friends. Then, they exercised the courage not to retreat in battle. They had a sense of justice so that they never would take a life without just cause, whether that life belongs to an enemy soldier or to an insect.

The code of conduct evolved into what we call the **Eleven Commandments of Taekwondo:**

1. Loyalty to your country
2. Respect for your parents
3. Faithfulness toward your spouse

4. Respect for your brothers and sisters

5. Loyalty toward your friends

6. Respect for your elders

7. Respect for your teachers

8. Never take life without a just cause

9. Have indomitable spirit

10. Have loyalty toward your school

11. Always finish what you begin.

These commandments are still taught daily in Martial Arts schools and are a direct reflection of generations of Taekwondo practitioners. It is from these eleven axioms that the five tenets of Taekwondo evolved. Respect and moral values have existed throughout the history of Taekwondo. It is up to the Black Belt to continue the legacy by demonstrating respect to everyone he comes in contact with.

The Martial Arts philosophy reflects a lifestyle of high standards that begins with respect. First, respect for ourselves, followed by respect for those closest to us, then all others, and finally, respect for our environment, which is, after all, an extension of ourselves.

Self-Respect

Self-respect is key in personal development, and is related to self-image. Someone who has self-respect will also have a strong self-image. Someone who is unhappy with himself will have less self-respect and in turn will have a poor self-image. A lack of self-respect often has to do with past experiences. We are who we are today because of the actions we have performed, the lessons we've been taught, and the experiences we've had. For example, an individual who has had a rough childhood may lack the self-respect and self-image of someone who has had a stable upbringing. Of course, there are many individuals from affluent backgrounds who have a negative self-image, and there are those who have defied the odds, growing up in poverty, and yet still became huge successes. It depends on self-respect and the conviction that one is worthy and can achieve.

Everyone has a story of some life-altering circumstance from the past. One's perception of those situations will determine how one feels about himself. Those who persist in living in their sorrows will lack the self-respect to move on. They may suffer from the illusion that they should remain in the pain they've endured in the past. That is neither true nor productive. Only if they can let go of the past and live in the present can they develop the self-respect that leads to a positive self-image. One of my mentors said, "The past is history, the future is a mystery and the now is a gift; that is why they call it a present." Focus on the present and be the best you can be in this moment. In other words, what happened in the past is gone forever; if you look at the past with gratitude because it brought you to where you are today, then it is all good. It is good to have goals and aspirations, but not at the expense of living in the future. The present is the gift that lasts for eternity, for if you are always mindful of what you are doing at any given moment, without worrying about the future or the past, which moment lasts forever. The ancient Buddhist philosophy of "mindfulness" reflects this idea. By being mindful of what you are doing from moment to moment, you are able to appreciate life.

Self-respect equals love and self-acceptance. In order to show others respect and love, you first must have it for yourself. What are your greatest qualities? Take five minutes and write down five reasons to love and respect yourself:

1. _____

2. _____

3. _____

4. _____

5. _____

If you found that difficult, don't worry. It's hard to acknowledge great things about ourselves. But no one is listening. You are not bragging. Just do it. This exercise in affirmation will plant seeds for future successes. Believe in yourself!

A Black Belt has developed the strength of character to love and appreciate himself. He has a sense of security that is conveyed in everything he does. Confidence and strength emanate from his being. He walks and talks with assurance. A Black Belt is trained to discover his own great attributes and will not fixate on self-criticism.

Here are ten exercises you could do to improve your self-image and gain greater self-respect.

1. Look in the mirror and repeat the five reasons you love and respect yourself.

2. Dress up one day and treat yourself to something nice.

3. Take a walk in the woods and breathe in the fresh air.

4. Watch a lovely sunset and appreciate its beauty.

5. Eat healthful foods and know that you are putting goodness into your body.

6. Practice deep breathing and imagine that with every inhalation you are bringing yourself positive energy, and with every exhalation you are getting rid of anything stale, toxic, or negative.

7. Call someone you haven't heard from in a long time and tell him that you were thinking of him.

8. Do a random good deed for a stranger and see how that makes you feel.

9. Do one thing NOW to look and feel better.

10. Look at everything, whether good or bad, as an experience that you can learn from.

By following through with even one of these exercises, there's no doubt that you will see yourself in a more positive light. Visualize how you would feel if you had the self-respect you deserve. If you see yourself in a positive light, you will inspire others to do so too. That is the Black Belt way!

Having self-respect you will be able to show respect toward your family and those closest to you. I have five children. When they show respect towards me and my wife, our home is harmonious. But when they display disrespect, you can only imagine the turmoil we go through. The other day, my daughter Kimberly said those dreaded words: "Shut Up!" to me. It took every ounce of Black Belt character not to spank her bottom. Needless to say, she went to bed early and without dessert. She did learn, in that episode, the importance of showing her parents respect. When another of my kids demonstrated extra respect by volunteering to help out and using good manners, he was rewarded by being allowed to stay up a bit later to watch TV. We all know what it feels like to be disrespected. Not so good. No one wants to feel "dissed."

In the Martial Arts School, respect is the foundation of everything we do. Respect is taught as soon as a prospective student walks through the door. He is greeted with a bow and "Hello, ma'am" or "Hello, sir." Our bow has a deeper meaning than simply showing respect to a person in front of us. As we bow, we put our hands together. The right hand represents our family and the left represents our friends, to symbolize our love for family and friends. Putting our hands together also strengthens our connection to the one standing in front of our heart. Conceptually, in front of us are our seniors; we promise to follow their lead and pass on the knowledge that has been handed down to us. Behind us are our juniors, whom we promise to lead by our best example. We say, "Thank you, sir" or "Thank you, ma'am" to show respect and appreciation for whomever we are facing, because without him or her, we cannot commence with our training. Since we have cultivated an environment of trust, there is no need for us to look the person in the eye. All of this takes place in the three seconds it takes to bow.

In class, students will bow before and after any technique they perform. They also will bow at the beginning of partner training, when students face each other and say, "Thank you, sir," to show appreciation for training with that partner. When an Instructor or Master asks students to perform, and even in conversation, students will respond, "Yes, sir" or "Yes, ma'am." It is up to us to continue the traditions that were handed down from Master to student for thousands of years. At the beginning of our training, we show deference not only to the Master, but to the seniors as well, to respect their rank.

It is also equally important that the instructors treat the students with respect. Bowing is a sign of humility, equality and respect. I believe that everyone is the master of some field, just as my expertise lays in the Martial Arts and in personal development. So everyone deserves respect for his or her accomplishments, and in this way, the show of respect is mutual.

And respect must be shown to all the members of one's family. Do you know someone who is nicer to strangers than to their loved ones? To me, that is completely backwards. It is those closest to you whom you should take care of first and love and respect most. Friends come and go, but your family will be there forever. Life is one huge, endless training session. When you become frustrated with someone you care about, figure out a way to maintain respect for him, as you resolve the issue. A Black Belt is always and everywhere in training.

The other day I was purchasing something at a store. The clerk was obviously bored, and greeted the customers mechanically and dully. I decided to conduct a little case study. When it was my turn to pay, I approached her and politely said hello. I got her usual minimal response. As she processed my purchase, I saw that her name tag read "Carol." The transaction complete, I did something that probably no one had done to her all day. I looked her in the eye and said, "Thank you, Carol, have a great day!"

Surprised, she met my gaze and said, sincerely, "You have a great day also, and thank you." Her tone of voice had changed, her posture straightened, and she was smiling. All because I took 30 seconds to show her respect. Imagine how many people go through life interacting with others without showing enough respect even to acknowledge them as fellow human beings.

The most challenging and stressful time of my life was when I was building my commercial building. I was using about 5,000 cell-phone minutes a month to call the bank, the attorneys, the builders, and the subcontractors, as well as everyone else in America and their grandmother. That day, I was at a local health food store picking up my lunch, and at the same time I was on a very important call from the bank. As I paid for my sandwich, I got the sense that I was being rude to the cashier by being on the phone. So I went back and apologized. Not because I had to, but because I felt bad that I hadn't paid her respect at that moment.

A Black Belt trains to be aware of his surroundings. Awareness is key in the Martial Arts, not only to check for possible danger, but to see how to improve or enhance one's surroundings. If you take 30 seconds out of your day to look someone in the eye in a friendly manner, you will make him feel respected and appreciated. Small gestures of respect can make a dramatic change in someone you interact with. Since we all live through our emotions and our feelings, if we act to make someone feel better, that could put him in a whole new frame of mind. The smallest show of respect has the power to change lives. By taking a step beyond what is expected, you behave like a Black Belt.

Respect for our environment is an extension of respect for ourselves. During the past decade or so, public awareness about the importance of protecting our fragile environment has grown. We are living in "The Green Era," and most people are conscious of how important it is to keep our environment healthy. The subject of "green" is everywhere: at the supermarket ("Bring your own bags to reduce plastic!"), the bookstore (where entire sections are devoted to books on "going green"), the hardware store (where you can find "green" products galore), on the internet (countless websites about recycling, global warming, solar energy, and climate change, etc.). I appreciate this awareness, and hope it does make a significant and positive impact on the environment.

I am a supporter of former Vice President Al Gore and his work to highlight the harm we have done to the earth. In his documentary, *An Inconvenient Truth*, Gore explains the reality of global warming and how it will affect our future and our children's future. For over a hundred years, industry and technology have been growing at an exponential rate. So many people and industries are using up our natural resources, polluting and wasting resources as if they owned the earth. Little do they know that the damage that is being done will be catastrophic to the next generations. If we simply cleaned up after ourselves, as we were taught to do in kindergarten, life for everyone else would be so much more pleasant.

Another daunting fact is how fast technology is advancing. A better, faster computer comes out before you get used to the one you had just bought. We are in the smartphone era, and computers are portable and tablet-sized, and fit in the palm of our hand. The technology way of life is causing major learning challenges for the youth of today's culture. Many children, used to and dependent on texting, are deficient in communication skills. When it comes time to apply for a job, many will not have sufficient interpersonal skills to do well in an interview.

Social media has many benefits, such as reuniting people who have been lost or estranged – but the benefits come at the expense of a lack of personal communication. I absolutely love technology, and embrace the fact that it is here to stay. My hope is that it will not impair the environment, and that the innovators, who are changing the way people do things worldwide, show enough respect for the environment to keep it safe for future generations.

Speaking of the environment, in the Martial Arts

School I suggest that students spend as much time outdoors as possible, especially in the woods. The natural energy there is so powerful that a tree, which has grown from a seed, has the power to split a rock in two.

In this picture, the bottom arrow points to a tree root that has grown into a rock. The upper arrow shows how the root has kept growing through the rock; in the space between the arrows, you can see that the tree actually has split that rock in half. Amazing! This phenomenon is present all around us. If only we could tap into that natural power source, we would be unstoppable at whatever we want to accomplish in our lives. But no one can tap into that natural power if he doesn't respect and appreciate its source.

There is an enjoyable movie starring Matthew McGonagal called *Failure to Launch*. Here is a very successful guy with a lot going for him, and he still lives at home with his parents. His parents want to get their grown son out of the house so that they can have their own life. Throughout the film, the young man is attacked by all kinds of usually benign animals: a dolphin, a chipmunk, a lizard. Since the guy is out of harmony with the universe, the universe lashes back at him.

When you are not respecting the environment you dwell in, it will not respect you. Take time to enjoy the outdoors, learn to cherish it, and respect its pleasures and gifts. You will gain tremendous benefits, such as peace of mind and appreciation, not to mention the gift of fresh air! You will be in sync with nature. And you'll remember that you are part of nature, too.

On a hike recently, I was with a Martial-Artist friend. At one point we saw a whole family of deer just across the path from us. My friend slowly walked up to the deer, and instead of bounding away in fear, the deer started moving toward him. That was a very rare thing to witness! Animals are sensitive to our manifestations, whether they're calm or angry and tense. If they sense danger, they will flee. Because my friend was so tranquil and steady, the deer not only were unafraid of him, they allowed him to come close to them. All because of his Black Belt mentality and his appreciation of and respect for the environment – his attunement with nature.

By showing respect and appreciation for where we live, we will become aligned with the environment and can embrace its priceless gifts. The Black Belt practitioner works closely with his surroundings, respecting all around. In return, the environment continues to supply endless opportunities for us to experience its beauty and wonder. Respect breeds respect. This is most evident in Mother Nature, and the entire world we live in.

"Knowledge will give you power,
but character respect.**"**
BRUCE LEE

"Respect your efforts, respect yourself. Self-respect
leads to self-discipline. When you have both
firmly under your belt, that's real power.**"**
CLINT EASTWOOD

CHAPTER 8

PERSEVERANCE

We are in a large high school gymnasium in beautiful, mountainous Pennsylvania. The Black Belt candidates have endured an arduous weekend retreat that has challenged them physically, mentally and spiritually. They have been going strong since their arrival on Friday evening, when they began their first vigorous, three-hour training session. The next morning they were up at dawn and did not stop until 11:00 that night. Now it is Sunday morning, and exhausted, they are looking forward to graduating to Black Belt by demonstrating hundreds of techniques in self-defense, free spar and the difficult "breaking" process.

There are both male and female students of all ages, from seven through seventy. They have trained and practiced over and over again to hit the boards with a striking force. Despite their fatigue, their energy is flowing to the max. The only obstacle before them now consists of three boards and a slab of cement. They go through the first break flawlessly. For the second one, they break the board into three pieces with precision. They step up to the cement break, a little uncertain, not knowing what to expect, since they have never before broken cement. They turn around and announce to the audience at the top of their lungs, "I AM GOING TO BREAK THIS BRICK." They look at the brick; snap their hands back to their sides, and say, "YES," and again, "YES." Raising their arms to blast through the brick with a palm strike, they give the loudest *kihap* ever and hit it with all their might. The brick doesn't break. There is a huge sigh in the audience, and the students don't know what to do. In their minds, they did everything correctly: they did the positive affirmation, they busted their move, and they used proper technique. So why didn't the brick break? Again they repeat the process. Still it doesn't work. A third time and then a fourth, but still, the brick remains intact.

After observing the challenge and struggle of the break, I walk up to one of the students and joke, "What's going on here? I thought the brick was supposed to break." The student looks back with a frustrated smile and replies, "Yes sir." I ask him to take a deep breath and close his eyes, to regain his center and his focus. I remind him that he does have the ability to blast through this brick. The ability is deep within him and he must truly believe he can do it. For this defining moment, he must pull from resources he didn't know he had. Gradually my voice becomes more intense. I urge him to visualize the brick blasting underneath him, to believe in the desired outcome, and to make it happen! He replies confidently, "YES, SIR." Twice I ask, "Are you ready?" Twice he replies, "YES, SIR." He approaches the brick again with confidence, chambers his arm up, explodes it down and the brick splits in two. He jumps into the air, along with everyone watching, and gives me a big hug, and then he starts crying with joy. He defied the odds and broke the brick. That, my friends, is real perseverance.

This true story occurs at every Black Belt graduation we host. When a student cannot break a board or a brick, I actually get happy, because in my experience, authentic development and inner strength grow not when things are going well, but when you are forced to dig down deep within yourself to reach your potential. My delight comes from the fact that the student becomes stronger by overcoming adversity. People benefit on many different levels through perseverance. It gives them the opportunity to achieve what they had set out to do, and, more significantly, it gives them a greater sense of accomplishment, which in turn transfers into confidence. Finally, perseverance allows them to achieve things in life that most people only dream of.

Perseverance gives you the opportunity to accomplish goals that you set out to do. So many people start a project and never finish it. For example, when I started training in the Martial Arts, over twenty-eight years ago, it was said that only one percent of students achieved Black Belt. Out of nearly a hundred people who began their training at the same time I did, I was the only one who followed through. Today, an estimated twenty-five percent of students are expected to achieve their Black Belt; an improvement from years ago, but most students still do not follow through to the goal of Black Belt. Why? Because they lack perseverance.

This goes for college graduation as well. According to the Department of Education, thirty percent of college students drop out after their first year, and fifty percent after their second. It is said that only half of the students enrolled in college have the perseverance to graduate. If the ones who drop out had had a never-give-up attitude, they would have found a way to graduate.

What about people who settle for a job they don't really like? Can you imagine waking up every morning and having to spend eight hours doing something you hate? To me, those individuals lacked the perseverance to pursue their dreams and desires. A Black Belt will not give up on his dreams. He will realize what he loves to do in life and will run with it. That is Black Belt perseverance. He will persevere until he lives the life he chooses to live, not one that he must suffer through.

This is the formula for the Perseverance Principle:

Perseverance = Confidence = Success

Through perseverance, one overcomes obstacles and accomplishes a task or goal, and that translates into confidence. Confidence is crucial for achieving any level of success. It is a necessary attribute for Black Belt students in training; especially when they approach the cement slab at the end of their graduation ceremony! Confidence gives you the conviction that you can make anything happen. Attaining confidence, you will be able to demonstrate it throughout your life. Whether you are in school or working, being with family and friends, or spending time alone, confidence will take over your whole being. You will walk with a certain presence, yet not need to be noticed. Having inner peace and pride within, you will have no need to show off.

Bob Proctor, a famous public speaker whom I had the opportunity to train under, uses a term that resonates in my being: "Calm Confidence." Grandmaster Byung Min Kim teaches me and the other UMAC Masters that one should never get *overly* excited, upset, happy or sad; we should stay as close to our center as possible. A tendency toward emotional extremes is counter-productive and can be destructive. One who emotes excessive euphoria will doubtless also experience excessive depression. A Black Belt has the ability to maintain calmness. When you match a calm persona with the confidence that comes from perseverance, anything is possible.

Here's a personal example of perseverance. I undertook the project of a lifetime in 2008, directly after a three-year effort to fulfill my dream of building a commercial building for my Martial Arts school. I had to use every ounce of Black Belt character to make it happen, and at the forefront of my arsenal was perseverance. The two bankers involved were actually amused by how many obstacles I had to overcome. One banker shook his head and referred to Murphy's Law; whatever could go wrong certainly would go wrong. The other said he'd never seen anyone take so many hits and keep going. I said that I'd fought the best fighters in the world, and I'd prefer to confront them again, than to have to deal with the challenges I was now facing with this building project. What really amazed them was that every time I chalked up another obstacle, I was smiling.

About three years ago I had a vision of constructing a building for my Martial Arts school. My longtime training partners and closest friends had purchased and renovated the buildings they were operating in. I was teaching in three separate spaces in the same building. One space, 2,200 square feet, was located on one side of the building. Another thousand square feet was located downstairs and only accessible by going outside. To get to the third space, which was 2,600 square feet, we had to walk through a day-care center, a vet's office, and a hair salon. I paid three rents, three electric bills and three of every other expense. To say the least, this was an extremely inefficient way to run a business.

On the main drag in the community there was a 5,400-square-foot building for sale. I tried for it, but was outbid for a cash deal. Then I found the last piece of vacant land in the area; it would be a great property on which to build my dream school. After six complicated months of touch and go negotiations, a deal was struck. Then came a long series of obstacles.

The first major obstacle was that the amount I thought I had to pay was $75,000 less than what was actually required. I'd assumed that every dollar I'd put into the project would count towards the down payment, and I found out that only certain items such as architectural fees and preliminary construction fees qualified, while fees such as attorneys' fees, consultant fees and planning board fees, among many others, did not count. What to do? I was out of funds and the owner was threatening to withdraw the deal if I didn't get everything done by a certain date. I contacted a company that lends bridge loans, to borrow the money and repay them at the end of the project. Three days before the closing, on a holiday weekend, we had to come up with $75,000 or lose the deal. OUCH!

I called my wife and my program director into the office and said we had to raise $75,000 by Tuesday or the deal was off. I said I already knew every reason this would be impossible, and that all I wanted to hear was how we'd make it happen. We came up with a solution; we would sell lifetime memberships for $10,000 each, we would ask students to advance their tuition, and we would double the length of their membership from six months to a year. We emailed and called every student, and managed to come with $74,989.11 – just $10.89 short! What an unbelievable moment! But just as we were congratulating ourselves, there was a second obstacle.

We'd come up with $75K, but now we were told that we needed *another* $75K. Not again! The Small Business Association needed us to finish paying all of the down payment (which I thought I had already done), and wouldn't allow us to start construction until we did. The steel structure had been delivered to the property and was just lying there in pieces. So I scrounged around some more, and again was able to pull a rabbit out of the hat. Luckily we had a hefty tax return, and we also borrowed from a private lender, and against future collections of tuition. Relieved, we started construction, assuming our hurdles were over. Wrong!

The third obstacle presented itself. We began construction just as oil prices peaked to an all-time high. As a result, all of the sub-contractors increased the prices of everything the builder had estimated. We ended up twenty percent over budget, which caused another financial challenge. Again I had to figure out what to do. My solution this time was to finish the building myself. I did all of the finish-construction; I put up walls and sheetrock, did the taping and baseboards, erected the ceilings, and everything else. Our building was finished, but not without the ominous presence of a 12-foot-tall, blow-up rat, compliments of the Union and its picket line, which tried in vain to halt the job. Good going, until the fourth obstacle arrived.

This obstacle was a delay in opening the Martial Arts school. It should have opened in September, and we weren't able to open until January. We had to consolidate three spaces into two and lost about twenty percent of our enrollment. We promoted a grand opening for December 1st, since our other leases were up and we needed to move out. The building department would not give us the Certificate of Occupancy and we could not move into the new space. I lost another ten percent of our enrollment, and we operated out of the local high school at $200 per day. Yikes.

There were many more obstacles and challenges to overcome, and narrating them would be a book in itself. My purpose in telling this story is to show that when you have an important dream, you will do whatever it takes to make it happen. It took tremendous perseverance to make this building a reality, but I am happy to say that we are in the building, the students are happy, and the numbers are growing every week. Many people went above and beyond to help make it happen, and we are extremely appreciative of all the efforts. They say that sacrifice means giving up something of a lesser value for something of a greater value. In this case, the ideals and the dreams of having the ultimate training facility for my students far outweighed any personal challenges I had to overcome. Going through this experience gave me extra confidence and I know that there is nothing I can't accomplish. I attribute my Black Belt mindset to this success, which has given me the perseverance to see my goals through.

The Black Belt practitioner has demonstrated perseverance time and time again when he learns a new pattern and remembers to execute techniques extremely well. Perseverance is demonstrated regularly as students work hard kicking until they feel like they can't kick anymore, and then do ten more. Perseverance is seen most prevalently at Black Belt graduations, when students try to break a cement slab which doesn't break so easily. The students persevere by stepping back, taking a deep breath, finding an inner strength they didn't even know they possessed, and blasting through it.

Perseverance is the ability to follow through with a goal, dream or aspiration and overcome tremendous odds in the process. Let's list a few individuals who overcame huge odds to achieve success.

In order to create a light bulb, Thomas Edison made 10,000 attempts. When asked about it, he replied that these were 10,000 ways *not* to do it. That is perseverance. Bethany Hamilton, a teenage surfer, lost her arm in a shark attack in October 2003 and returned the following year to take fifth at the Nationals. That is perseverance. And did you know that Michael Jordan, the greatest basketball player ever, was cut from his high school basketball team? I bet that coach is feeling a little silly right about now. Another example: the guy who thought up the idea for FedEx (which is now imitated by many other companies); that is, to route all parcels through one hub, wrote it as a Master's thesis and only got a C. Bet that professor is feeling a little silly as well! Or how about the seven-year-old who comes up to speak in front of 200 people, and who attempts to break a piece of cement with his hand? When it doesn't break the first time he finds the inner strength and perseverance to hit it harder and break it. Perseverance is within all of us. Each one of us has the ability to keep pushing forward if the outcome we want is important enough.

❝The brick walls are there for a reason. The brick walls are not there to keep us out. The brick walls are there to give us a chance to show how badly we want something. Because the brick walls are there to stop the people who don't want it badly enough. They're there to stop the other people.**❞**

RANDY PAUSCH, <u>THE LAST LECTURE</u>

CHAPTER 9

ATTITUDE OF GRATITUDE

We are at a United Martial Arts Center [UMAC] Dragon's class. A group of four and five-year-olds sit around our dry erase board. The instructor asks the question that is posed at the beginning of every class: "What do you think is important to a Taekwondo student?" The children raise their hands eagerly. One of the boys is called upon, who answers, "Self-control, Sir." The instructor smiles and points to a second child, who says, "Try your best, Sir!" The instructor tells both boys, "Great job," and writes their responses on the board. He asks a third child, who replies, "Integrity, sir." The instructor asks, "What does integrity mean?" The student answers, "To do your best when no one is watching, sir!" The instructor writes the answer on the board, and then calls upon a little girl with her hand raised. She says, "An attitude of gratitude, sir!" The instructor nods and smiles. "Great job. And what does that mean?" The child says, "To be grateful for everything we have, sir!" The instructor nods. "And what are you grateful for?" The little girl responds, "My family and friends, sir!"

The class continues with their lesson and the instructor rewards the students by sending them to the board to put their name on the virtue or value they had listed. This is how we encourage students to become aware of and practice Martial Arts character. It will be some time before they earn a Black Belt but there is no need for them to put off acting like one.

Teaching the importance of gratitude starts with the first lesson. We teach students how to bow, and show them what bowing represents. Bowing is recognized as a sign of respect all over the world. The deeper the bow, the higher level of respect you are expressing. Bowing also displays humility. A Martial Artist will have no problem bowing to someone because he has a firm sense of security within himself. He enjoys letting others feel appreciated by bowing to them. I am a sixth-degree Black Belt in Taekwondo and have absolutely no problem bowing to a four-year-old white belt who comes to the school for a trial lesson. I consider bowing a privilege.

To review the technique of bowing, we hold out the right hand, which signifies family. Then the left hand, which signifies friends. When we put our hands together, close to the heart, we are indicating how important family and friends are. In front of us symbolically we show gratitude towards our seniors, teachers and higher belts; behind us we show gratitude for the opportunity to lead our juniors and lower-ranking belts. The students will bow without needing to meet his partner's gaze, because he respects and trusts him. The student yells out a confident, "Thank you, sir." This expresses gratitude and appreciation for the teachings of the instructor. If they are partnering with another student, they will be showing gratitude and appreciation for having a partner to train with. In response, the instructor or the partner will bow back, saying "Thank you, sir" or Thank you, Ma'am." This happens twenty to thirty times during a class, because respect is the foundation of the Martial Arts. We tie gratitude to respect every time we bow. We know that to achieve what we desire in life, we must have the Attitude of Gratitude.

No matter how hard one's life seems, there are others whose lives are much harder. I came across this statement recently: *"If you have never experienced horror of war, the solitude of prison, and the pain of torture or near death starvation, then you are better off than 500 million people."*

Wow, that is powerful. When you read that, you will think: I guess it's not so bad that I didn't get that new car I wanted. There is a universal law called the law of relativity. Everything in the universe is just is. There is nothing good or bad unless it is related to something else. There's an old story about a man who cried because he had no shoes, until he met a man who had no feet. Can you see how powerful gratitude could be in your life? To go a step further, the law of vibration states that everything in existence is made up of energy and has a vibratory rate. The denser the item, the faster the molecules will go and the more tightly they move together. The law of vibration is like the law of attraction, which states that *like will attract like*; if one thing has a particular vibratory rate, another thing with the same rate of vibration will be attracted to it. Did you ever notice that when two drops of water lie next to each other, they will pool together into one drop? But if you put a drop of oil next to a drop of water, they won't merge. Their opposing vibratory rates keep them from combining. Here's how gratitude enters into this law.

When you are in a grateful state, you are in a particular rate of vibration. You will attract things to you which vibrate at the same rate. Gratitude produces a positive vibration that will attract positive things to your life. On the contrary, if you maintain a mentality of poverty and envy, emphasizing what you lack, you will continue to repeat the experience of scarcity over and over again. It is crucial to live with gratitude and appreciation to go far in life and experience all that you desire.

Having Black Belt discipline will help you train your mind to focus on the attitude of gratitude every day. The Black Belt perspective on life is to appreciate everything around us, from the air we breathe to our family and friends and all other blessings. Notice how people who habitually complain always have something to complain about, while people who are grateful tend to have a lot to be grateful for. Black Belts will find the positive in all opportunities. In chapter two, we talked about negative and positive people. I am sure you can figure out which are filled with gratitude and which are filled with envy. A Black Belt mind finds the silver lining in every challenge. He will be grateful for that challenge, for the opportunity to become stronger. Let me give you an example from my own training.

Grandmaster Byung Min Kim has been teaching me and the other UMAC Taekwondo masters about the more spiritual side of the Martial Arts, through meditation. I have gained great benefit from his life-altering teaching. He encouraged us to do longer and longer meditation sessions. The other masters and I experienced quite a bit of pain, sitting without moving for long periods. For example, a foot might fall asleep and I'd either lose all feeling in it, or it would cramp painfully. One time we were all having tea with Grandmaster Kim, and I asked him about this obstacle. He smiled and said, "Good for you, you now can be grateful for the pain that you experience, and that will keep you focused." He was right. As we continued our training, we were able to maintain the position for a lot longer with minimal discomfort. That lesson can be applied to everything we do. Grandmaster Kim teaches us that we must focus consistently on improving and being grateful for our accomplishment, and then we will be able to accomplish anything in life.

Remember, the more you are grateful for, the more things you will have to be grateful for. This is exactly how we teach our students to live happier and healthier lifestyles:

This month we are focusing on gratitude as our theme. Every day could be the best day in your life. By showing gratitude to those close to you and for the things you have in your life, your life will be more meaningful and significant. We tend to overlook the little things in life that make us feel great. For example, could you imagine not having a car to get around in? What would you do? How would you get to class, to school or to work? How often do you reflect on how fortunate you are to have the means to be driven to or drive to your destinations? Wow, we are really lucky! What about the parents who drive you to all of your activities? Have you shown appreciation for all that your parents do for you?

Here is an exercise that will help you get into a positive state of vibration and help you to reflect on how lucky you are to be you.

First, look inside yourself to see why you are so lucky. List four things that you are most grateful for:

1. _____
2. _____
3. _____
4. _____

Now list four people whom you are most grateful for having in your life, and why:

1. _____
2. _____
3. _____
4. _____

Finally, list the top three opportunities, activities, events, or clubs that you are involved in, which you are most grateful for.

1. _____
2. _____
3. _____

Isn't it obvious how lucky we really are? Every day is an opportunity to make someone else's day by showing another individual the appreciation you feel for him. It could be a heartfelt hug for your parents or child, or it could be looking a cashier in the eyes and saying thank you with a smile. In these small ways, we enlighten other people's lives. That is the role of a Martial Artist in our society and that is his obligation. Show those you care for how much you care about them.

No matter what state of mind you were in before you did this exercise, you are likely to feel a little better now. This is something you can do all of the time. I can't begin to tell you how many people gripe about all the things that are going wrong in the world. If they would only shift and find something that is going right, it would open up a whole new perspective on life and they would have more things to be grateful for.

There's a woman in my school who is an instructor under me. Her two children attend the local school. This family has been members for many years and has shown tremendous dedication to the Martial Arts and to our philosophy. At one point, she was having a challenge with her eight-year-old son, who was acting up in school and being disrespectful to everyone. The boy was preparing for Black Belt. I wanted to see what was going on with him in school, to cause him to act this way. In my opinion, behavior is a symptom of some deeper cause. My thought was if we could find why he is acting this way, we could come up with a reason for his behavior.

The mom set up an appointment with the teacher, an assistant, the school psychiatrist, the child, and me. I walked in and after the traditional pleasantries; I turned to the child and asked, "What's going on?" He was very shy as I expected he would be, and I hoped the teacher would offer some positive words about him. Instead, the teacher lashed out and verbally battered the child with everything he was doing wrong: he doesn't listen, he talks back, I can't work with him, etc. When this litany of abuse was over, I said to the teacher, "Now please tell me what he is doing right." That flustered her, and her assistant then chimed in with nice things to say about the boy.

I think that boy's biggest problem was his teacher. If the teacher had found the small things her student was doing right, this conflict never would have happened. I like the saying, "Attention goes where energy flows." In this case, the teacher was putting her attention to what the boy did "wrong," so she received the same negative energy back in the form of poor behavior. If the teacher had approached the boy out of gratitude for his good attributes, or for the opportunity to help him, the outcome would have been different.

A Black Belt mind would have been grateful for the chance to help someone in that situation. In fact, he would put more energy towards him with the attitude "whatever it takes" to make things right. Live with the Attitude of Gratitude and you will live a much happier and more fulfilled life.

" *There are only two ways to live your life. One is as though nothing is a miracle. The other is as though everything is a miracle.* **"**

ALBERT EINSTEIN

" *You have no cause for anything but gratitude and joy.* **"**

THE BUDDHA

CHAPTER 10

WHO'S IN THE DRIVER'S SEAT?

Now that we have learned about the five tenets of Taekwondo and how they can be applied to everyday life, let's spend some time focusing on who is in control of one's success. I remember teaching a Martial Arts class on this topic to a room full of Black Belts. The discussion was triggered by a student in his early teens who was blaming his parents for not preparing him for class with a proper uniform. He was in a pair of jeans and a t-shirt with his belt tied around his waist; they were the same clothes that he had worn throughout the school day. I am definitely not a stickler for students to come to class perfectly dressed in the proper uniform – it's far more important that they come to class at all. To this kid, I privately joked, "Hey, Joey, nice uniform!" The boy mumbled some excuse that he'd forgotten to bring his uniform. I said, "How could you forget your uniform?" He replied, "It's my mother's fault. She forgot to pack it for me." Ah, here was a perfect opportunity to teach the class about responsibility. Of course I never would single out a student in front of a class to make him feel bad, but when given the opportunity to teach a valuable life lesson, I don't hesitate.

I sat the whole class down to talk about taking the importance of taking responsibility for one's success. I emphasized how crucial independent practice was; reminding them that I would not be there at all times to protect them. What would happen if, God forbid, they had to defend themselves against an attacker? It is up to each of you, I said, to practice hard and develop enough skills to be able to defend yourselves on your own. I explained, "You are in the driver's seat; you have complete control of how great a Martial Artist you become. It's not up to me, or your family. It's up to you and you alone." I paused, making sure I had everyone's attention, then said emphatically, *"Who is in control!"* They replied with equal force, "Me, sir!" "Exactly," I affirmed.

I pulled the student who didn't have uniform off to the side and asked him about it again. He gave me the "I-get-the-point" look and said that it wasn't his mom's fault and he himself was responsible for not being in uniform. I said, "Good job," and gave him a high five and a bow.

I think one of the biggest challenges these days is that we have enabled one another not to have to take responsibility for ourselves. We've talked about the Law of Attraction, where a person attracts everything in life that happens to him, whether good or bad. It is much easier to blame others for negative situations than to take responsibility for them ourselves. No one else can be blamed for something negative that happens to you. Once we realize that, we can change the way we go about things and work to attract the good things we aspire to.

As I write this book, we are coming out of the worst economic situation since the Great Depression of the 1930's. So many people have lost their jobs, their houses, and often their dignity and sense of hope. Although there certainly are circumstances beyond our control concerning unemployment (as when a company is forced to downsize), the exceptional people manage to keep their job or transfer to a new department in the downsized company. It is the exceptional employee who takes responsibility for his success at the job and whom the company wants to keep.

At a seminar I attended recently, the speaker said that the reason this economic situation is so challenging for so many is because so many companies have been forced to let go of "good" people. During economic crises of the past, companies would let go of average workers who did not show great effort at their job, while the hard workers stayed on. Today, however, it is the good people who are being let go and the exceptional people who still have work. Therefore, for one to keep his job secure, he must be not merely good, but exceptional. And being exceptional means to choose to take responsibility for being excellent. Thomas Friedman wrote a book about globalization called, *It's a Flat World After All.* In it he warns young people that if they are not exceptional in their education, they won't merit the jobs that hard-working students in third-world countries will win by virtue of their sense of responsibility, ambition and professional excellence.

I am not in any way minimizing that current economic situation and do not intend to offend anyone. My focus is to emphasize that among the many choices everyone must make in life, an important one is to stay in the driver's seat of their own car, as difficult as that often is. But commitment and responsibility surely will drive them to success. If you let someone else drive your car and expect to go in the direction you want, it never will happen until you jump into the driver's seat.

Obviously, when a student becomes a Black Belt, it is he and only he who physically executes the moves. No Martial Arts instructor can perform them on his behalf. What instructors can do is help students realize their abilities and help them believe that they can succeed. We can all live by this philosophy. With a Black Belt attitude, you make sure you are in control of your world. You own your thoughts, and these thoughts will determine how you feel. How you feel will determine how you act, and how you behave ultimately will determine your success. With a Black Belt mind, one can control his thoughts, which determine, finally, the results of any situation or endeavor.

"*If you can learn to motivate yourself, you can always tap into an abundance of energy that will drive you to the success you dream of.***"**

RACHAEL BERMINGHAM

CHAPTER 11

BLACK BELT PRIDE

Have you ever seen someone who is a master at his field? Did you ever take the opportunity to appreciate the workmanship that went into a fine piece of handmade furniture? What about the attention to detail of an artist who has just completed a masterpiece? Have you ever watched a professional dancer deliver a peak performance? Or best of all, how about a Martial Artist who is going for his Master Instructor Certification, who is executing each and every move with precision, grace and power? All of these examples exemplify Black Belt Pride.

Black Belt Pride is a state of being that is part of any task done with great attention and care. I have been fortunate to travel three times to Korea, the homeland of Taekwondo. It was incredible to experience the cultural background of the art that I've devoted my life to. I noticed a big difference between how the Korean and American cultures regard work. Most Koreans have profound appreciation for their field and work hard to become a master in it. Once Grandmaster Byung Min Kim took me and the other UMAC masters to a master tailor to get traditional suits called honboks. The tailor was a short, stocky man who didn't speak any English. Of course, he was well dressed in a honbok like the ones he was known for creating. The custom-made suit is loose-fitting and extremely comfortable; we wear them at our Black Belt graduations and traditional tea ceremonies. He came to our hotel room to take our measurements, and he had with him a small notebook, a pen, and a tape measure. He took a few measurements and jotted them down in the notebook. He then looked at us and entered something else in the book. He did not ask what color or style we wanted, he chose for us. When we received our custom-made honboks, they were exactly the right size and they exactly matched our coloring. The precision and care that went into our suits was magnificent.

Of course there are master craftsmen in our culture in every field of expertise, but not nearly as many as there are in Korea, where even the most ordinary job is done with extreme respect and seriousness. Employees in Korea are more like apprentices. For example, in restaurants, the cooks, chefs and waitresses all evinced a sense of pride in their work. In our culture, few people have that sense of pride in what they do. Often Americans work just to pay the bills, without any pride or appreciation as I have seen in Asia. I think that the main reason for this disparity is that in our society, most people work for money; in Korea, they work for gratification, which is reflected in the quality of the job that is done. Our society tends to want to get paid more for minimum work. There is an undertone in our culture, especially among the young, that says, "What can you do for me?" This attitude is backwards. It should be, "I will work hard and do the best job I can, and I will earn my success."

We teach the same principle of pride in whatever we do, both in and out of the dojang. Being a Black Belt is about excellence in all areas of life, not only when in training. For the kids, it is equivalent of working a little harder to get that "A" on the test. It is doing more than what is required to demonstrate that you care about what you are doing. When you do the best you can, you hand in a project with a sense of pride and accomplishment. That pride will take the child to unlimited possibilities in the future.

For adults, it could be a project related to their profession. You make sure that you don't just get by, merely by taking the easy way out, but by doing it the right way. This goes for taking pride in raising your children. You make sure you do the right thing rather than the easy thing. Demonstrating your pride to your children sets the best example for them. Action speaks louder than words, and if you take pride in your actions, your kids are likely to follow suit. Take pride in your relationships, especially with those most important to you. Freely express that you love them and are proud of them. Take pride in everything you do.

Taking pride in something is a state of mind that is directly connected with your personal standards. The higher your standards, the greater effort it will take to achieve the sense of Black Belt Pride. On the contrary, if we set low standards for ourselves, we will not experience as much satisfaction. To find out if you have held yourself to high standards and whether you have the right to be proud of what you have done, ask yourself questions such as:

Have I done my best?

If you feel that you did not do your best, ask yourself another question:

What could I have done better?

In this case, you need to be a good finder to find the positive in the situation. After each class, during the final meditation, I ask the students to evaluate their performance in the class they just took. Had they done their best? If so, they deserve to feel proud of their accomplishment. If not, they should ask themselves what they could do next time to feel proud of their experience. Then they must commit to trying their best the next time. We always ask the students to do a self-reflection and spend time assessing ways they can improve. If we all did this exercise throughout our lives, and took the opportunity to learn from everything we did, we'd all continue to grow.

We've talked about the Universal Laws throughout this book. Another principle is the Law of Polarity, which states that if you are not growing, you are deteriorating. A tree, for example, either will get bigger or will deteriorate and die and ultimately turn back into soil. If we are constantly negative, we deteriorate until we have no self-regard left, then it is only a matter of time until the physical body registers the toll of this psychological negativity, and becomes ill. If you approach every challenge as a learning experience, you will turn it into a growing opportunity. You will become smarter and wiser than before. This is turning a challenge into an opportunity, which means having a Black Belt mind. Have you ever noticed how inspiring it is to talk with older people? I could talk to an elder for hours, drinking in all the experiences he or she has lived through, especially if they've become the master of their own life. That is why in eastern culture, the elderly are so revered and respected.

Recently, one of my 14-year-old Black Belt students got into some trouble at home. He was misbehaving, being extremely disobedient and defiant at home. He had started years before in a program that we have for individuals with special needs. He made tremendous progress in his training, excelled in the program and became mainstreamed into the regular classes. Not many people believed that he would be able to reach Black Belt. Despite his accomplishments, he had this issue with his mom that failed to demonstrate Black Belt character. I called him into the office to discuss it. I began by explaining that I was aware of the situation and was not angry or disappointed in him, but that I'd like to help him resolve it, to prevent something like this from happening again. I explained there is more to being a Black Belt than having achieved a high level of physical ability. A Black Belt represents the Five Tenets, too. I asked him if he thought he'd demonstrated respect, perseverance, integrity, indomitable spirit, or self-control. When he said he hadn't, I said that now we knew where he went wrong.

I gave him an assignment to do before his next class. I asked him to list the Five Tenets of TKD and explain how he should have incorporated them into the situation he'd gotten into trouble with. This way he could establish a new plan if the issue were to occur again. I reminded him that a Black Belt is most impressive by how he behaves outside the school, how he presents himself, and the qualities he expresses that define him as a Black Belt. Having him write out a plan for how he would have applied the TKD principles would give him a winning way to handle whatever problem, challenge or confrontation he may face.

The goal is to apply the Tenets in everyday circumstances to achieve success and happiness. Doing so will create a win-win-win combination. A win for you, because you will have disciplined your mind and followed a system that leads to a positive outcome; a win for the other side, when you show the Martial Arts qualities of respect, integrity and self-control and a win for the Martial Arts school and staff, because you have represented the values that we stand for and earned our pride. I was going to recommend that the teen tattoo the values on the back of his hand, but I don't think that his mom would have approved!

At the end of the day, having Black Belt character is defined by one's actions. If you go through life using the Five Tenet philosophy, a positive outcome is practically guaranteed. For people who are new to making this effort, avoiding the easy way out may be a little difficult at first. It's much easier to sit on the couch and eat Doritos than to go to Martial Arts class. If you take the time to process the Five Tenets to see which ones apply and how to utilize them in any given situation, you will find the positive outcome. Try it and see what happens. The greatest asset is to be proud of who you are. In making the effort to be genuine and conscientious, you will attain Black Belt Pride.

Here is an exercise that will let you apply the Tenets in your life. After writing this out, put it in a safe place as a reminder to follow the values.

Write down a situation that was in some way unfavorable to you.

_____

_____

_____

What was the outcome of the situation? _____

_____

_____

_____

Write down how you could have handled the situation by using the Five Tenets:

Integrity

_____

_____

_____

Self-Control

_____

_____

_____

Perseverance

_____

_____

_____

Indomitable Spirit

_____

_____

_____

Respect

_____

_____

_____

Now, write down the outcome that you think would have happened if you had engaged the Tenets: _____

_____

_____

Finally, say out loud: *I am happy and grateful for applying these Black Belt principles to all areas of my life.*

66*Do not go where the path may lead, go instead where there is no path and leave a trail.*99

RALPH WALDO EMERSON

CHAPTER 12

GRANDMASTER KIM'S FOUR PILLARS

My Grandmaster requested that I teach a class called Dah Do, which is designed to enhance the spiritual aspects of the Martial Arts. He asked us to give a deeper meaning of the Martial Arts to our students, with the idea of passing on the knowledge that he has given us. I start the class with some light stretching and proceed to the Ki Exercises, which combine flexibility training with deep breathing exercises. We then spend a good portion of the class practicing a simple and very beneficial focus meditation. After the meditation, during the traditional tea ceremony, we discuss how to apply the Martial Arts principles to our everyday life.

During one session, we talked about what Grandmaster Kim called the Four Pillars to Enlightenment. Each pillar represents an area of life that one should develop to achieve inner peace and harmony.

The first pillar is to **eat healthfully**; using more living foods like vegetables and fruits, and avoiding processed foods such as chips and chicken patties. The great health aficionado

Jack La Lanne, who lived a long life of extraordinary vitality, said it best with, "If man made it, don't eat it." Grandmaster Kim also recommends a vegetarian diet, and I've embraced this for many years. There are philosophical and psychological implications to food choices. When a person is angry, toxins are released into the system that will create acids that will manifest as disease. Disease is nothing more than the body trying to rid itself of an excessively acidic condition. When an animal is slain for food, whether a cow, a chicken or a fish, toxins are released into their system; when we eat the meat of an animal, we also are consuming the toxins that were released when it was killed. Without meaning to generalize, it is not hard to visualize the temperament of someone who lives on steak and other red meats. Their nature tends to be more aggressive than that of a vegetarian, who tends to have a calmer demeanor.

Another concern about the meat that is produced today is that the animals are pumped with antibiotics to counteract the poisonous bacteria in their feed. Cows that are bred for milking are injected with such a high level of hormones which is causing our children to mature much younger than ever before. If you want to eat meat, please buy it at a health food store and choose only hormone and antibiotic-free products. Eating less meat and more living foods will give you more energy and calmness. I recommend the book *Food Revolution*, which discusses the advantages of a vegetarian diet over a meat eating diet.

The second pillar is that we should practice **meditation**, the key to tapping in to a higher power that will allow you access to more energy than you can imagine. Meditation slows the brain waves and relaxes the mind. A relaxed mind allows energy to flow through you. Life energy, called *prana* in Sanskrit, *Chi* in Chinese and *Ki* in Japanese and Korean, is like a water hose. When the hose is kinked, the water will trickle out slowly. When the kink is released, the water will flow effortlessly. In our lives, the kinks are fear, doubt, frustration, and stress. Tension and negative feelings release toxins into the system. Meditation gives you the chance to unkink your hose and let the energy flow through you.

This flow of energy will be expressed through ideas that will come to you in a relaxed state. At our seminars, I ask the audience when they have their best ideas. Most reply, "In the shower." I ask them why they think that is so. They answer is that in the shower they're completely relaxed, in seclusion from the stresses of the world, with the warm water trickling over them. I explain that everyone has the ability to experience an increase in ideas if they can relax their mind. And that is one of the functions of meditation.

A simple meditation that you can practice is what Grandmaster Kim calls a focus meditation. You breathe using your lower stomach rather than your chest. When you ask most people to take a deep breath, they fill their lungs with air and then exhale without engaging the diaphragm. The oxygen stays in the upper chest area and descends. As you breathe in through your nose, you are filling your lower stomach area with air and pushing it out and forward. As you exhale, your stomach area will come back in and the air will exit through your nose. Try it a few times. It will feel like you are doing backwards breathing. It is unfortunate that we are taught to breathe incorrectly. When I was at the doctor's for a check up, I was told to take a deep breath. I inhaled as I do in meditation, and the nurse said that I was doing it "wrong." I then had to fill only my chest with air. I started chuckling, thinking that she needed to practice meditation.

All I do in my meditation is count my breaths. Each inhalation and exhalation counts as one complete breath. I continue to count in my head, focusing only on the counting. If I want to do a half hour meditation, I will count from 1 to 100 and then count backwards from 100 to 1. If I want to do an hour I will go from 1 to 200 and 200 to 1. Now, here is the important part. Ideas and thoughts will come into your head throughout the meditation. It is extremely important that you do NOT resist them. Don't pay any attention to those thoughts. Allow them to come in freely, and as quickly as they come in, they will flow out again. Sometimes you may have an epiphany or breakthrough, in which case you can stop your meditation to write it down before continuing. Many ideas have come to me in meditation. The idea for this book came during a meditation. Practice by starting with short segments and build up to longer periods. I guarantee that you will receive tremendous benefits! Stop reading and practice ten breaths right now.

The third pillar that Grandmaster Kim teaches us is about drinking **green tea**. This is not any tea like you could get from the grocery store. This is a wild green tea that is grown on the rocky slopes of Mt. Jilee, in Korea. The roots of the tea bushes go down into the earth as far as 50 feet, and assimilate the best of the earth's nutrients and natural energy. The temperature differential from morning to evening is greater than what you would find in the northeastern United States, even in summer, which leaves a stronger "Chi" or "Energy" in the tea leaves. The tea bushes are grown in the wild and not on commercial plantations. The wild green tea is hand picked, processed, roasted and bagged within a 24-hour period, which ensures its freshness.

There are many benefits associated with drinking green tea. Below is a brief insert from the brochure of a teahouse in New York City called Franchia. It is the only teahouse that sells the Korean Royal Green Tea.

All teas contain polyphenols — naturally occurring compounds that are effective antioxidants for disease prevention and treatment of many health-related illnesses. But, the level of polyphenols in Green Tea is higher than Oolong Tea and Black Tea. Because Green Tea is unoxidized, these unaltered polyphenols are its primary active ingredients and as a result, its health benefits have been documented by numerous scientific researches. Green Tea has proven to lower cholesterol, reduce blood pressure (lowering the risk of heart attacks), aid digestion, fight fatigue, preserve younger-looking skin and prevent dental cavity and gingivitis. Recent animal studies have shown that green tea extracts protect against cancers of lung, breast, prostate, liver, skin, esophagus and colon.

The tea is to be used in conjunction with meditation. And there is a proper way to drink the tea when you are in a group, a process that we call *Dah do,* or "The way of Tea." This beautiful ceremony allows you to fully embrace the present moment and share something special with others. The server sits down first and everyone else follows suit. Traditionally, we sit on the floor with our legs crossed. We keep silent as the server pours hot water into a cooling bowl. He or she will then pour the hot water into all the cups to warm them. The cups of water will then be poured into the teapot and allowed to steep for thirty seconds. The server then pours the tea into another bowl for rinsing the tea leaves before serving. He pours another bowl of hot water and waits for it to cool. The correct temperature is ascertained not with a device like a thermometer, but merely by placing the hand on the side of the bowl. When the water is ready, the server adds it to the teapot and lets it steep. The tea will be poured into each cup, filling it about a third of the way. After all of the cups have been poured, the cycle begins again. By circulating the pouring of the tea like this, the strength of the tea will be the same for each cup. During the process, the server is careful not to spill water or tea. When finished, he bows to the tea to show appreciation to nature for providing the tea for the company. The guests bow to the tea for the same reason. The tea should be swallowed in three sips. The first is swished through the mouth to embrace the flavor. The teacup is gently and silently put down, and the process begins again with the next serving. You have five servings per session, and each gives the experience of a slightly different taste. As the servings continue during the ceremony, the leaves open up and release the energy stored in the tea.

The tea ceremony gives a special value to shared time. There is no greater gift than the gift of time that you give someone you care about. It is better than any material thing that you could ask for. Dah do is an opportunity for just that, to be present and in the moment, which ultimately creates a meditative environment. I highly recommend that you give it a try. You will gain a greater appreciation for the important things in life. As I am writing this now, I am drinking tea the same green tea I have been describing to you. Oh yes, another great benefit is that drinking green tea gives you mental clarity, which will help you find the best solution in any situation.

One time I was doing a seminar at a Girl Scout convention and I offered to host a Dah Do session at 6:00 in the morning. It was definitely early for a lot of folks, but about ten people showed up. Some of them I hadn't met before, except that they'd come to the morning meditation and to have tea. As we were having our tea that morning, one person mentioned a way to spread the health benefits of tea to more people. Then another person had an idea and a third and fourth person had ideas, and next thing we knew, we had a whole business plan to start a new tea business globally! We didn't act on our plan, because all of us were happily busy in our lives. The point was, a group of strangers, sharing green tea in a relaxed state, experienced a flurry of ideas that spread among us like wildfire. I explained why this had happened, and they completely understood.

Energy has the ability to flow to and through us in many different ways. Some ways will be through physical exertion, some will be through mental exertion. When ideas flow like that, you increase your mental energy, which is where those great ideas come from in the first place. That is why mastermind groups and work study groups are so beneficial as long as they are in the right environment. All this from a few cups of tea.

The fourth and final pillar that Grandmaster Kim has taught us is to do **random acts of kindness** to others throughout the day. Doing good deeds will have a lasting effect on family and friends as well as on perfect strangers. The idea is that doing a good deed makes someone else's day a little brighter and more positive, which will make them a little happier and more positive. They will go home and share that same positive feeling and energy with those they come in contact with, and it will be a huge ripple effect that could spread throughout their personal circle. That one good deed might ultimately have a positive effect on hundreds of others, creating a happier and more positive community, and a happier and more positive world.

I have taken this concept a step further in my Martial Arts school. I teach that as a White Belt, a beginning student has the responsibility to perform one good deed for another person. It doesn't have to be anything major; in fact, it could be holding the door open for someone or pulling out a chair for them to sit down. In other words, it involves simply doing some act of kindness to make another person's life easier. For Yellow Belt students, they will be responsible for doing two good deeds per day. Every rank requires one additional good deed. A Black Belt is responsible for doing ten good deeds every day. Second-degree Black Belts do twenty acts of kindness; third-degree Black Belts do thirty, and so on. Getting into the habit of doing a few good deeds a day will make them associate their training and Martial Arts responsibility with performing good deeds routinely. Then they will make a positive impact on society and the community by doing those selfless deeds on a regular basis. That's pretty awesome.

At one Dah Do session, I was explaining the four pillars to my students, elaborating on Grandmaster Kim's teachings and going deeply into the lifestyles of a Martial Artist. In this particular session, one of the Dah Do students present was the mother of one of the Black Belts. She works in New York City and takes a train to the subway every day, often during rush hour. One day, she took her son to the city on "bring your son to work day". As she was exiting the subway, a man in front of her dropped his briefcase and all his papers and belongings flew all over the place. Everyone was stepping over the man's belongings as he struggled to gather his things. No one helped him. Even the mom, who was locked into her own preoccupations, stepped over the mess and continued onward. My student tugged on his mother's arm and said, "Mom, we should help him." They both turned around and helped the man, who expressed his appreciation before they parted ways.

The mom came to me the next week and told me the story with mixed emotions. She was both happy and disappointed. Happy and proud that her son had the fortitude and the selflessness to stop and help the stranger in need. She was very grateful that we had taught her son about the importance of doing good deeds and that her son lived up to our expectations. But she was disappointed in herself that she hadn't thought to stop and help the man. It was a lesson for her about awareness and about seeking out opportunities to help others. For me, it was a double positive, for one of my Black Belts was living up to the standards I set for him, and it was an additional positive that the mom is now more aware of doing selfless deeds and the importance of the impact it could have on others. She learned a very valuable lesson from her ten-year-old boy. But not just any ten year old, a Black Belt!

Let's imagine the rest of the man's day after he'd dropped his briefcase. If no one had helped him, he might have trudged through the day wondering why no one had stopped to help him. He may have complained bitterly to everyone he knew about his bad luck. Then, because of the law of attraction, his negativity would have attracted other negative events throughout the day. At home, he would have complained to his family about the incident, and by the end of the day, he would have worked himself up into a miserable state.

But because the mother and son helped him, I think it's likely that the scenario worked out to be very different. He would have told the story of altruism at work, and at home, his mood would be happy. He'd feel great to be a New Yorker, and would go to bed contented.

One year my wife and I took the children to the historic Navy ship *Intrepid*, docked in New York City. We stopped to get a bite to eat and my wife Kathy left her purse on a bench. We'd gone all the way up to the flight deck of the USS Intrepid before she realized she'd left her purse. Of course, we feared that her purse was gone for good. She left the ship to look for her purse, but in vain. Then a woman from the snack shop we'd been at came out and handed my wife her purse. She said someone had seen that it had been left there, and brought it to her, in case someone came back for it. Nothing in the purse had been touched. My wife was so happy and appreciative; she went around telling everyone how great New York City was and that there were still good people out there.

Can you see the power that doing good deeds can have on someone? What I have not yet touched on is the power of doing good deeds that the person doing them will have. There is a great sense of pride when you do something nice for someone else. For me, it is one of the greatest gifts to know that you made a positive difference in someone else's life. It is definitely why I do what I do and even why I am writing this book. If one reader takes away a little knowledge and is a little happier or a little healthier, I will have succeeded. When I do a seminar, my priority is to make a difference. If one person out of 100 or even 1000 has a more positive attitude, I am happy and I'd consider my seminar a success. Of course, the more people who are impacted, the happier I become.

When you have the ability to do a selfless deed, it makes you feel great knowing that you have made a positive difference for someone else. A Black Belt is someone who is willing to give without needing or expecting to receive. He does it just for the sake of giving.

Grandmaster Kim believes that following the Four Pillars will help one achieve a state filled with peace and love. He says that success is not defined by how much money you have or how much real estate you have acquired. Success is having "Forever happiness." When one has forever happiness, what else in the world will one need? Forever happiness is a state of being and a mindset that will determine a life filled with love and harmony. Who could ask for anything else? This will happen through an appreciation of the limited time you have on this earth and a drive to live life to the fullest. To seize every moment, from the time you wake up to the time you fall asleep, and take advantage of everything life has to offer.

"To enjoy good health, to bring true happiness
to one's family, to bring peace to all, one must
first discipline and control one's own mind.
If a man can control his mind he can find
the way to Enlightenment, and all wisdom
and virtue will naturally come to him.**"**

BUDDHA

CONCLUSION:

A BLACK BELT WORLD

Wow, we have covered a tremendous amount up to this point. You must realize by now that Black Belt is a state of being, a lifestyle, and a set of values to live by. I would like to paint a picture of what life could be like if everyone in our society lived by these values of perseverance, integrity, respect, indomitable spirit and self-control. Politics would be completely different, wouldn't it? What about crime, or underachieving? All of these things would not exist. Of course, these things will still remain, but if we change ourselves and impact others, we could leave a mark. Let's don our artist apron and imagine what our lives could be like if everyone lived in this manner. Imagine that everyone lived a life filled with integrity. What would life be like if everyone did the right thing even when alone or if people always did what they said they were going to do, all of the time? I am extremely confident that anyone who reads this book will live life in a more positive way.

As we have mentioned, the power of positive actions and their effect could make a dramatic difference in society. Let's play the scenario from the last chapter where my student encouraged his mother to do the right thing and go back and help the man who dropped his briefcase. We concluded that he would go about the rest of the day much more positive than if he had been ignored by the commuters around him. I believe that positive actions have a ripple effect. When one small positive action happens, it spreads to many others and that positive energy spreads more. That man most likely went to work acknowledging the good deed that had been done for him and let his co-workers know about it. There could have been a discussion around the coffee machine that morning that had a theme of, "Wow, there are some really good people here in the city," which spread a good vibe amongst the office. Now, there always is a negative nelly in every group who may have not been impressed. However, at least a few people would be touched by the act. It would give them a little spunk to their step or adds extra light to their day. They then go and talk to their family and friends about what this little boy and mother did for their co-worker. It raises their awareness about the benefits of doing good deeds.

Meanwhile, the man with the briefcase had a much better day than if he hadn't been helped. He goes home to his family and tells this wonderfully positive story of how the boy helped him in the middle of the busy subway. His family is touched by the story and everyone is in a better mood, and they are encouraged to help someone in need who has had a similar misfortune. They are a happier family, and this one event has restored their faith in the goodness of people. The man's wife and children change their mindset to be good finders and start looking for good things that they can do for others. Most importantly, though, is that their dinner is filled with pleasant discussion instead of accounts of all the things that had gone wrong that day. That is the power of positive actions – where young Blake's random act of kindness affected the man's co-workers in his office, his family and had spread to other circles of people. This is the way that you can spread Martial Arts values to others by doing good deeds without wanting or expecting anything in return.

Grandmaster Kim once said, "Give without memory and receive without forget." This has stuck with me for a long time. Think about it. "Give without memory" means that you are willing to give, but not expecting anything in return. You are only giving for the sake of giving with no strings attached. Many people give and expect something in return. There should be enough satisfaction and gratification simply in the fact that you made a positive difference in another's life.

"Receive without forget" means that when you receive a gift or a random act of kindness from someone whether it be your family or a stranger, that you don't forget it. Not only don't forget it, but remember how you felt when that good deed was done for you and let that be a driving force for you to help others to keep that memory alive.

When I hear the term "A Black Belt World," I think about a society that is a more positive place to live. Communities where respect and integrity are present all of the time and there is genuine care for one another. A place where people have trained themselves to look for and focus on the positive while regarding negatives as learning experiences. A Black Belt world is what I had been able to create in my Martial Arts schools where students are positive, genuinely care for each other and go out of their way to make others happy. I fostered this community so that when someone walks into my facility, the positive energy in the atmosphere blows them away. I often hear people comment about the positive energy in the Martial Arts school. It is my vision and ideal to bring that same atmosphere to masses of people to create a global Black Belt world! It starts small and begins with all of you. Develop the Black Belt mind and know that *it is not about the belt*. It isn't about the belt you wear, but who you become and your ability to approach life with self-control, respect, integrity, indomitable spirit and perseverance. When this is accomplished, success is inevitable, whether or not you are literally wearing a Black Belt.

Thank you for the opportunity to serve you!

ABOUT THE AUTHOR

Master Chris Berlow resides in Mohegan Lake, NY with his wife, Kathy, five children Brandon, Andrew, Timmy, Stefanie and Kimberly with dog, Kodiak. He owns, operates and still teaches at his Martial Arts School, United Martial Arts Centers in Briarcliff Manor, NY. His school has won numerous national awards including School of the Year by industry organizations. In 2012 he received the Best in Westchester prestigious award out of 117 Martial Arts schools in one of the most affluent counties in the United States. Master Berlow was a state, national and international competitor and was a five-time NY State Champion, two-time Junior Olympic Gold Medalist, Sr. National and U.S. Olympics Festival Bronze Medalist and Elite Open Silver Medalist. He continues to train daily and is under the tutelage of Grandmaster Byung Min Kim where he visits on a weekly basis.

Chris is a co-author of the Amazon Best Seller, *YOU Have Infinite Power*, which he wrote with Rick Wollman, Nick Palumbo and Master Paul Melella of Empowered Mastery. He travels across the country with Empowered Mastery giving seminars and coaching individuals to live with passion and purpose.

Master Berlow is an avid outdoor enthusiast who enjoys mountain biking, snowboarding and hiking. In 2012, he and his wife hiked the Grand Canyon to raise money for Leukemia. His favorite quote is from Henry Ford, "Whether you think you can or think you can't, you're right". Master Berlow has committed his life to help everyone believe that they could achieve anything they set their mind to and use that positive mindset to live a more meaningful and fulfilled life.

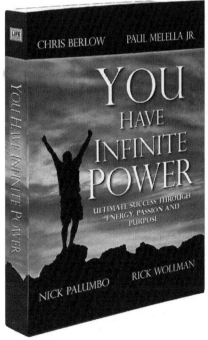

EMPOWERED MASTERY
Your Life   Our Passion   One Purpose

Inspiring you to think *UNCOMMONLY*

Empowered Mastery
Your Life Our Passion One Purpose
To inspire and impact professionals
and entrepreneurs to achieve
ULTIMATE success Personally,
Professionally, Spiritually and Physically
so they can live a life filed with passion and purpose.

Is there way too much negativity in your world?
Learn how to take control of your thoughts.

Are you tired and frustrated doing the same thing every day?
Learn how to love what you do for a living.

Have you lost your drive and passion?
Discover your true passion and purpose.

Are the toxic foods you eat slowly poisoning your body?
Learn to finally live a healthy and vital life forever.

www.empoweredmastery.com

Master Chris Berlow
is the owner and head instructor at
UMAC BRIARCLIFF
528 North State Rd., Briarcliff Manor, NY 10510
(914) 945-7100
www.umacbriarcliff.com

Respect

Discipline

Confidence

**In a
"Feel Good"
Environment**

For the very best Martial Arts training in your area,
please visit the following UMAC locations:

UMAC ARDSLEY
15 Center St.
Ardsley, NY 10502
www.umacardsley.com

UMAC CARMEL
114 Old Rte. 6
Carmel, NY 10512
(845) 225-0008
www.umaccarmel.com

UMAC FISHKILL
1054 Main St.
Fishkill, NY 12524
(845) 897-8622
www.umacfishkill.com

UMAC PARSIPPANY
164 Halsey Rd.
Parsippany, NJ 07054
(973) 515-0702

UMAC RIDGEFIELD
722 Danbury Rd.
Ridgefield, CT.
(203) 431-1432

UMAC WARWICK
153 Rte. 94 South
Shoprite Plaza, Store # 3
Warwick, NY 10990
(845) 987-1853
www.umacenters.com

GRAND MASTER B.M. KIM's
TAE KWON DO

White Plains	Port Chester
914-428-0085	914-934-1861
Scarsdale	Nanuet
914-472-2060	845-623-2002

www. bmkimtkd.com